ALL BRAVE SAILORS

A PENNANT UNIVERSAL,
    SUBTLY WAVING ALL TIME,
     O'ER ALL BRAVE SAILORS,
ALL SEAS, ALL SHIPS.

WALT WHITMAN
SONG FOR ALL SEAS, ALL SHIPS

ALL BRAVE SAILORS

The Story
of the
SS Booker
T. Washington

by

JOHN BEECHER

1 9 4 5

L·B·FISCHER · NEW YORK

ALL BRAVE SAILORS *By* JOHN BEECHER

Contents

AUTHOR'S NOTE

o   o   o

Thanks are due to COMMON GROUND *and the* NEW REPUBLIC *for permission to reprint material originally published in their columns*

Foreword

IN THE medieval world, men often concealed the heart of their faith in the crypts of their churches. Coming down dark, winding stairs you find in the shine of candles some glorious mosaic, some fresco bursting with life, or chiseled capitals spelling out a dream of hope. On the SS Booker T. Washington you climb down the long, steep engine-room ladder, gripping the hand-rails so nearly unbearably hot, down under the sea level. Then your feet are on the plates, polished and clean lifting and falling with the swell. You move to the chant of burnished, pulsing shafts in the rich odor of oil like incense, and you come on the painted medallions. They stand out on the clear aluminum color of the boiler fronts, warm as the roaring flames within. They are the vision of "Red" Herrick, a white artist who once tended these boilers as an act of faith and of love, risking his body in the perilous enterprise of war. Off watch, he spread out on the blank, tempting surface of his boilers the dream that filled him, the dream of brothers.

Booker T. Washington looks out from one, the sad but strongly believing face and the book he wrote, "Up from Slavery." A white hand shakes a black hand in another. Intent dark faces bend over desks, with books. Men climb, white and black together, up tortuous stairs, behind banners, toward shining habitations. Here is the secret of this ship, explosive as one of the big bombs in the forward hold on its way to blast fascism, more powerful than the pent-up steam in the high-pressure cylinder.

Whatever port we touched—for I was privileged for nearly two years to be a part of this ship, a citizen of this new world—we shook men to their foundations. Not by preaching, though we were sometimes accused of carrying on "agitation," but by simply being. Everyone had said it couldn't be done. Here was the living proof.

We who sailed under Captain Hugh Mulzac were no band of saints, no select company of fanatic volunteers, but just the common run of men. We were of all races—mostly Americans, though we included also Brazilians, Filipinos, Scandinavians, Spaniards, Persians, West Indians, Peruvians. Among us were white men, born and bred in the South, who took orders from Negro officers, ate and slept alongside Negro shipmates, went ashore in foreign ports with Negroes—and on occasion knocked down those who wanted to make something out of it.

I am still too close to the experience to connect everything up, and the war still imposes its limitations on what can be told, but these blank sheets, like Red Herrick's boiler fronts, seem to be made for medallions. . . .

CHAPTER ONE

Ship's Meeting

EVERY SUNDAY we hold a kind of service aboard the SS Booker T. Washington. We call it ship's meeting. We hold it in the officers' saloon. The fellows are perched all around the place in their dungarees and khakis, officers mixed up with men. On no other ship could you hold a union meeting in the saloon, for usually unlicensed men are forbidden even to set foot in it. On no other ship would you find everybody at the meeting, from the Captain down to the mess-boy. It isn't that there's no discipline aboard. On the contrary, it's out of these meetings, where everybody has his say from the mess-boy up to the Captain, that discipline flows.

Right now Harry Alexander has the deck. He's the ship's delegate. Each trip we elect one. This is Alex's fifth trip, and his fifth as ship's delegate. That shows what we think of him. Alex is a union

man, through and through. He helped to build the
National Maritime Union back in the rank-and-
file days. He took all that the shipowners and the
phonies in their pay could dish out. Once, in New
Orleans, the phonies nearly got him, riddling the
door of the office he was barricaded in with bullets.
But it was one of them who went to the hospital,
not Alex.

Alex is about as broad as he's tall, with gray eyes
like the sea on a stormy day, and hair like sedge in
the wind. He's about as solid as a man can be, in
all ways. Off his engine-room watch, when he's not
setting some guys straight about democracy and
unionism in a crew-mess session, he's flat on his back
in his bunk. Not asleep though. Reading. Good
books and bad, he reads everything new aboard
every trip, the good ones for mental ammunition,
the bad ones to get a line on how his enemies think,
and what they are up to now. These enemies he
lumps together under a single heading—"the phonies"—and he means by "phonies" all those everywhere who are out to get something for themselves
at the expense of the other fellow.

Alex has the deck at the meeting and he's blowing his top. Nearly the whole crew is new this trip,
and several of the guys haven't got the hang of what
the SS Booker T. Washington stands for. They
have been caught selling food to the soldiers we're
taking overseas in the 'tweendecks. More than five
hundred soldiers are aboard, and, since they aren't

working, but only traveling, the Army cuts them down to two meals a day. What with their salt-air appetites, the powdered eggs and canned hash they get at their two daily meals don't go far toward filling them up. The hungry GI's will pay up to 50 cents for a sandwich and almost any amount for a pie from the merchant crew's galley.

"What the God-damn hell," Alex bellows in his foghorn voice, "is coming off on this ship? You think you guys can get away with selling food to soldiers on here? You think this is just another ship? Who wants this ship to be just another ship? Is that what you all want?"

"No!" says everybody.

"I want you guys that have been selling food to soldiers to know that this is the Booker T. Washington," Alex goes on. "We don't sell any food to soldiers on this ship. These soldiers are our guests on here. Anything we've got is theirs, free. I'm telling you it's a big honor to this ship to be carrying these soldiers. They're our brothers in this war, and here some of you guys are trying to make money out of them. How are you going to feel about yourselves when you hear that some of these soldiers you sold sandwiches and pie to have been killed somewhere?"

Alex fixes his baleful gray eyes on the silent culprits in their corner—pretty decent guys, all three, who just hadn't thought. Maybe they figured their work in fixing the sandwiches or baking the pies was worth something. Bootlegging food is standard practice on troop ships, since they are all hungry ships for some military purpose or other.

"I didn't mean to sell the pie," says the Baker miserably. He is one of the best-liked men aboard, always doing favors for you, and he can really bake. His pies, doughnuts, cakes, and cinnamon rolls are the best you ever tasted. "Honest, Alex, I gave the soldier an extra pie and he handed me a dollar. I handed it back to him, but he made me take it for my trouble. It was just a tip."

"Just a tip!" says Alex scornfully. "We're going to start taking tips on this ship for doing what any decent guy would do? And you call yourself a union man! You used to be, maybe, but now you're phony, and you don't belong in the NMU. Brothers, I want to move that these guys who admit that they sold food to the soldiers or what they call 'took tips' be fined $50 apiece. I want to move further that they be brought on charges when we get back to the States, and kicked out of the union."

Alex's motion is seconded and the whole roomful of men is a single eye boring into the three accused. Captain Mulzac is recognized and gets up.

"I am ashamed for this ship," he says. You can see that he really is, and that furthermore this ship means more to him than his own life does. "I am ashamed for this ship," he repeats more slowly, and I remember all the nights he has gone sleepless to pull her through undersea danger—this frail brown man with the mild eyes behind his glasses, the always simple mien and speech. "This ship" it is invariably when he speaks of her, never "my ship" as with other masters.

"You fellows didn't know what you were doing maybe," Captain Mulzac says. "But I'll tell you what you were doing. You weren't just selling sandwiches and pie. You were selling the good name of this ship for a few miserable coppers. We have given this ship a good name all over the world. Everywhere people know about this ship. Millions of people are saying prayers for this ship, because she is a good ship, and they are praying that she will sail safely through all the war. Two of you fellows are Negroes. Do you know what this ship means to our people? Do you know how long we had to wait for this chance to show what we could do? Do you know something else, that this is one of the few spots in all the American war effort that isn't Jim Crow, where Negroes and whites and men of all races and nations get the chance to show how they really can work altogether in harmony? And to pocket fifty cents for a sandwich or a dollar for a pie you would kick all this away and give the people who want us to fail a chance to say, 'Well, the Booker T. Washington turned out to be just another ship, nothing extra at all. We knew it all the time.'"

The Baker, a Negro, is crying over in his corner. The other two men sit dejectedly, looking down at the deck. Chief Engineer Irving Smith gets up, a Negro powerful in mind and body, who never misuses his strength.

"Let's think about this, brothers," the Chief says, "before we are too hard on these boys. What they did is wrong. Alex is right: no good union man would do what they did. The Captain is right: they were selling the good name of the Booker T. Washington. But let's think back. I've been going to sea since the last war, and I remember how it used to be. A man had to chisel every way he could to live when they paid us only $30 a month, or even less—$1 a month for work-aways. A lot of seamen got the chiseling habit, just to live. They had to do it. Now we've got strong unions and decent conditions. Nobody needs to chisel any more. We can be self-respecting men. But some of us haven't waked up to that yet. We go on chiseling, just from habit. I think these boys have learned a lesson. Let's give them another chance. Let's fine them, because they deserve it, but let's not kick them out of the union."

"Can I say something?" The Baker is on his feet. "I know now I done wrong, brothers. This ship means just as much to me as she does to the Captain and the Chief and Alex. You all knows I done everything I could to make everybody happy. I baked you cakes and doughnuts and cinnamon buns and hot rolls. I let you have hot bread out of the oven in the middle of the night. And I gave lots of stuff to the soldiers, too. I baked it special for them, and I gave it away. I didn't want to take that tip, and I wish to God I hadn't. I'll pay any fine you say, but please, brothers, don't put me out of the union."

A vote is taken on Alex's motion, as amended by the Chief, and the three food-sellers are fined $50 each but not recommended for expulsion from the union. Then Ted, the Steward, gets the deck.

"The whole trouble," Ted says, "is that the soldiers aren't getting enough to eat. They're getting all the Army allows them, but two meals a day—the kind they serve—aren't enough. Now here's the proposition. There are only about seventy-five of us, including the gun crew, and there are more than five hundred soldiers. We're all eating well—eggs for breakfast every morning, fresh meat twice a day. If we gave them all we've got to last us the whole voyage, it wouldn't mean they could have fresh eggs or meat at every meal. What we can do, though, is give them half our eggs and half our fresh meat. That means we'd have to cut ourselves down to eggs just three mornings a week and fresh meat at only one meal a day. I want to move that we do that. And another thing. I want to move that we invite twenty-five soldiers to be our guests in the crew mess at every meal. The stewards' department will volunteer to cook the extra food and serve the extra serving."

Ted's motions pass unanimously, together with a motion from the Captain that five Army officers shall eat in the saloon as his guests at every meal. Then the Baker gets up again.

"The soldiers are mighty fond of pie, brothers," he says timidly. "Couldn't we do something about that? Nothing in the world I'd like better than cooking them pies for the soldiers."

A final motion adds a weekly serving of pie to the Merchant Marine's gift to the troops aboard, and the meeting is adjourned. When the Navy gun crew is polled, all those boys agree to share with the soldiers on the same basis as the rest of us. Next day we get the soldiers' response, an editorial written by a T-5 who edits the Army Page of our ship's newspaper, *General Alarm*. "MORE THAN DEMOCRACY" it is captioned.

"America, fighting to protest the democratic way of life, is sharing her guns and food with her less fortunate Allies.

"The Booker T. Washington does more than that!

"America, fighting to protect the democratic way attain the final goal—Victory.

"The Booker T. Washington tightens its belt to go much farther than that!

"Civilian America thinks itself horribly abused to go without prime cuts of beef and to be forced to walk.

"The Booker T. Washington grins and gives away a large portion of its limited supply of choice food.

"There is no need to ask why the crew of the Booker T. Washington—operative and protective, Merchant Marine and Navy—went so far as to share their food with the soldiers. The act can mean only that they believe sincerely in the American way of life. They could see no reason why some men should fare better than others when all are fighting for the same goal.

"Underlying the move was the National Maritime Union, typifying unionism and its 'sharing and brotherhood' at its best. The soldiers aboard have been amazed constantly at the *esprit de corps* of the men of the Booker T. Washington. Such fellowship is almost unbelievable. It goes deeper than unionism, deeper than race. It goes straight to the heart of the democratic spirit.

"So, men of the BTW, as long as there are soldiers to talk and pass on their experiences, the Booker T. Washington will live. This simple act of yours will reach well around the world—told and re-told as an example of the true spirit of co-operation.

"Please accept these thanks, pitifully small. The soldiers will not forget."

Nor will the Booker T. Washington forget these soldiers, with whom it was our privilege to share. We delivered them safely to a Mediterranean port, where most of them—together with the T-5 who wrote that editorial—were put aboard a big transport bound for India. She never got there.

CHAPTER TWO

Moment of Silence

W HEN I FIRST JOIN the SS Booker T. Washington, I assume—as most landsmen do—that there will be a ship's doctor aboard. I discover that all the medical care we shall collectively have during the long weeks at sea, among all the dangers from disease or accident or enemy attack, will be what I can give. I, whose knowledge of medicine consists of a semester's freshman hygiene course in college, and whose practice extends no further than putting band-aids on blisters and Unguentine on burns, am the "ship's doctor," nurse, and pharmacist combined. Just on the side. My main duty is serving as purser, the officer who attends to the ship's business and records.

We are just out of port when an oiler is brought up from the engine room with his right hand a bloody, pulpy mess. He had been feeling the main bearing of the high pressure engine, to make certain that it wasn't overheating, a delicate operation with the engine going full speed and the shaft rotating, but it was his job to do it. A heavy wave hit the ship on the quarter just as he touched the bearing. As she shuddered and rolled, he lost his balance and his fingers were drawn into the eccentric. It doesn't look as if much is left of them.

This oiler's name is Antonio Plaza-Blanco. He's a Spaniard. He makes no fuss about his hand, just looking at the mess of it, with his very white teeth bared and clamped tight. He has seen much worse than this in his time, short as it is. He's only twenty-five now but he first went to war at seventeen, as a Spanish Loyalist soldier. He fought through three years of it, and was at Almeria, Malaga, Teruel, Valencia, and the siege of Madrid, where he was badly wounded by a Nazi aerial bomb. When he got well, he was promoted to corporal and assigned to a shock brigade, an outfit that was sent to the hottest spots in the line for attack or last-ditch defense. He was captured in the final collapse and put in a concentration camp at Sevilla. By day he worked on the construction of a big airfield for Franco—perhaps the one from which Hitler's JU-88's later took off to bomb our ship near the Spanish coast, just missing us and crippling a ship in the next column.

Three sides of the airfield where Antonio worked were hemmed in by charged wire with armed guards patroling it. The fourth side was made by the Guadalquivir River. One day when he was working close to the river, Antonio made a dash for it. He got across, with bullets singing and splashing around him as he swam. Hiding by day in the homes of the people, and walking toward the sea by night, he reached La Linea, opposite Gibraltar. There he hired a rowboat, ostensibly to fish in the bay. He rowed clear over to Gibraltar, and was free.

All the while I work on him in my crude way, Antonio makes no complaint. He must know his right hand is at stake. But he leaves it up to me and luckily I have sulfa. They finish the healing in the Army hospital on the other side, saying he couldn't have come through in better shape, and Antonio stands all his watches on the homeward voyage.

The job on Antonio is my breaking-in as "ship's doctor." The next job is tougher. Our Steward is a Negro named Bradshaw, standing about five feet four and weighing not less than three hundred pounds. He is probably the best-feeding Steward on the seven seas. Turkey every week, chicken and tenderloin steak twice, roast beef, ham, lamb, and the primest of chops the rest of the time. Wonderful soups every noon and salads for supper, the best breads and pastry, and always enough of everything for a "full-house," a "come-again" or even thirds if you want.

No doctor on earth would pass Bradshaw except for the most sedentary shoreside work. No doctor has passed him. Men go to sea these days without even a cursory medical check-over. Seamen are scarce and, to keep the ships sailing, anybody with sea experience is acceptable. Later on, they will institute a system of perfunctory medical examinations for all seamen before they sail and will even give ships' pursers (including me) the rudiments of medical training. But not yet. Bradshaw is so fantastically overweight he can barely make it up the companionway from the 'tweendecks where his stores and coolers are; he is well over fifty and not feeling so good. After work this evening he sits out on No. 4 hatch with a few of his men, watching the sun go down over the warm quiet sea and the convoy like toy ships on a pond. It's hard to believe subs are all around, on such an evening. A cutter got one yesterday about this time, the gush of white spray and black oil bursting up from the depth charge just a few hundred yards astern of us. I saw it from my station on one of the after guns.

It is on the morning after that quiet evening that they call me in to see Bradshaw. He lies there, mountainous in his bunk, and the harsh rush of his breathing fills the small cabin. For three days and two nights I am in there with him, except for short spells, dosing him with aspirin and amytal, trying to keep him in his bunk. Every morning we flash over the blinker to the nearest escort vessel, a Coast Guard cutter with a real doctor aboard, asking for medical advice. The escort flashes back, "Administer sedatives. Absolute bed rest." But the sedatives don't seem to help. When the pain gets too intense to bear the huge man forces his way out of the bunk against my restraint and sits in a chair, fighting for breath with his eyes bulging. He thinks it's acute indigestion, but as it goes on day after day I know it must be something far more serious. There are too many subs in the vicinity for the cutter to break the radar screen around the convoy and come alongside to send the doctor aboard. That would take time, the maneuvering and putting over a boat. Not only would the cutter have to drop out of convoy, but so would we. A lot of lives to risk to save one. They aren't risked, and all the three days of terrible agony Bradshaw suffers, he never once asks for a doctor.

Sitting up with him, I learn a good deal about him. He is too sick to talk much. It is all he can do to breathe against the pain in the pit of his stomach. But the men who have known him long keep coming in to see how he is, and they tell me about him.

Bradshaw is a real old-timer, a seaman all his life until just the last years before we got into the war, when he retired to run a little restaurant in Harlem he had bought with his savings. But, after Pearl Harbor, the call went out for seamen ashore to come back and he came, though he didn't have to at his age and in his shape. He came back when the Nazi subs and planes were knocking off our ships faster than we could build new ones. He asked for the most dangerous run of all, to Murmansk. Off the North Cape his ship, together with most of the others in that convoy, got it. Bradshaw was picked up from the Arctic and, after long months on the beach in Murmansk with nothing to do but fight fires from the nightly Nazi air raids, was repatriated via Iceland. As soon as he hit the States, he shipped out again, for England. This is his first trip on the Booker T. Washington.

His friends also tell me his Spanish story. Bradshaw was for two years Steward aboard a Loyalist blockade-runner, bringing munitions into Barcelona, first from Marseilles and then, after the "non-intervention" pact closed Marseilles, from Odessa. Down the Aegean, up the Mediterranean, and through the narrows between Sicily and Africa where Mussolini's subs lurked waiting for them, close to Majorca and Minorca where Hitler's planes were based—again and again they made the daring run and came through every time. Bradshaw's ship was in Barcelona harbor when the Nazis pulled off their test of mass bombing, the rehearsal of what they later did to Warsaw, Rotterdam, and Coventry. That is one of the few things he has enough breath left to tell me about.

"I saw a school they hit," he gasps. "The school was in session. There was no warning before the planes came over, and no air-raid shelters like now. I saw them taking the children's bodies out. They took out five hundred children's bodies." He stops talking and props himself on his elbows, struggling for air. Then he whispers, "I can't forget it. When anybody says fascism all I see is rows and rows of children laid out with their arms and legs and heads blown off, and people still bringing more." He falls back shaking all over, this American Negro whose dying eyes still are fixed not on his own suffering, but on that of a people of another race, who fought for all mankind.

The end comes the next evening, right after supper. In a spasm of intolerable pain he jumps suddenly out of his bunk, staggers a few steps and crumples. For a long time we kneel over him, keeping up artificial respiration, but it is no good. I go up on the bridge, where the blinker has at last flashed an emergency call for the doctor. The cutter sweeps toward us from her flanking station. Our engines are cut, and on all sides the convoy is moving past. And now the cutter puts over a boat. It heads toward us, astonishingly small, swooping down and climbing up the swells against a blazing sunset.

The doctor's post-mortem judgment is swift. "Coronary thrombosis," he says. "Acute heart disease. A man in his condition had no business at sea."

It's a good thing Bradshaw can't hear this young medical officer in his brand-new naval uniform saying that he had no business at sea, he who had been sailing before the doctor was born, who was fighting fascism when it was just a word to most of us, and who died fighting it just as truly as if he had been wiped out by a torpedo-burst. But let Alex, the ship's delegate, speak for all of us.

"This Steward was a good-feeding Steward. And don't any of you first-trippers think that isn't important. If you're on deck or in the black gang down below you may think you're better than a guy in the stewards' department. You're wrong. Feeding is the biggest thing about a ship. Just let a ship start feeding bad and, no matter how good a ship it was, it's a hell-ship from then on.

"Let me tell you something else about this Steward. He was a union man. He was one of the rank-and-filers that built this union. He fought to get the kind of conditions you have today. When the time came, he fought fascism too. He didn't have to go to Spain, but he knew that was his fight and he went. He didn't have to take the Murmansk run, but he took it and got torpedoed. He didn't have to come out here to die this trip, but he came. He was a Negro and he knew his people weren't getting their democratic rights at home, but that didn't stop him from fighting this war against the guys that will take everybody's democratic rights away from them if they win out. I move we all stand and observe a moment of silence for the Steward."

He isn't buried at sea, for we are nearing port. We carry him ashore in the rough box Chips made for him, with the American flag covering it. A couple of Army trucks take us all out to the military cemetery where the Americans who fell in the landing here are buried. Like them, he lies there now under a plain white cross. This is the continent his forebears came from, shackled in the holds of slave-ships. Close to here a few weeks ago, two great democratic leaders met and forged the resolve to end slavery all over the world forever, to fight on against the slave-powers until they surrender unconditionally.

We get back to the docks where already the Negro GI stevedores are swarming over the ship and pulling out our cargo—bombs, surgical instruments, trucks, tanks, airplane parts, barbed wire, and bandages. Rest easy, Brother Bradshaw. We'll keep bringing more till all the world is free.

CHAPTER THREE

Chips

Down in no. 3 hold, Chips is building what he calls a punt. Now a punt is a little flat-bottomed boat you put over to paint the ship's side when she's at anchor or alongside the dock. But this thing Chips is building resembles no punt in all the annals of seafaring. We go down into the 'tweendecks and stare incredulously at the huge ribs of the thing Chips is hammering on. It looks more like the bare bones of old man Noah's creation, as shown in the Sunday school cuts, than anything else. When the skipper sees it, he blows his top. Everybody chimes in.

"Have you got davits and a lifeboat for it?"

"Where you going to put the radio shack?"

"She'll draw 30 feet—in 30 feet."

"Will it go through the hatch when you want to get it out?"

"It'll take a Caesarian to remove it."

"Christen it the Booker T. Junior."

"Hell, we'll have to use the Booker T. to paint Junior."

When Chips gets through, he has embodied a great dream. The punt has turned into a new-style lifeboat, entirely enclosed against the weather, with bunks below for the sick or injured, and ample room for stores. Unfortunately she lacks any means of propulsion but Second Assistant Engineer Treskin suggests that twin Packard engines can take care of that difficulty.

Chips has dragged himself out of his bunk, ulcers and all, to leave this memorial of his three trips on the Booker T. Washington. Nothing stops him, not the rough kidding, not the gigantic seas that nearly upset his ark upon him one day. He's getting off after this trip for a long rest, for he has at last come to see that he must.

Every ship's carpenter is called "Chips." But for those of us who sailed with Fred Reed, there is only one. Whenever we hear the Mate shout for "Chips," his image will spring to mind, swinging down the deck with his piratical gait, spitting Copenhagen snuff juice, the hammer looking like a toy one in his huge fist. It's no wonder Chips gives thought to the improvement of lifeboats. He has spent enough time in them, what with seven torpedoings. Three times he got it in the last war and four times in this one, twice on a single convoy to Murmansk.

They were off Norway when a squadron of Messerschmitt torpedo planes ducked down through the overcast and came in stack-high. Chips was on a 50-caliber and picked off one himself. But another came weaving through the fire and sent a torpedo square into their engine room. The fellows who were left, Chips among them, jumped into their rubber "zoot-suits" and piled off in a hurry.

"What you guys want?" a sailor yelled over the side of the next ship when Chips's boat got alongside.

"We're coming aboard for coffee time!" Chips yelled back.

"Like hell you are!" the sailor hollered. "Get clear there. We're coming off ourselves. We just got a torpedo on the starboard side."

Chips's boat rowed over to another ship and they were taken safely aboard, only that afternoon the

Messerchmitts pounced again and that ship got it.
She went down so fast they couldn't launch the
boats. Chips spent half an hour in the Arctic in his
zoot-suit before a British warship fished him out.
Another twenty minutes would have finished him,
for fifty was the number of minutes it took you to
freeze in that water, even in a rubber suit. Though
he is Irish mainly, with some Welsh, Chips is
swarthy enough for a Turk. He was in on the Casa-
blanca landing and did pass for an Arab in the off-
limits Medina, with a burnoose over his dungarees
and a red-tasseled fez. If only the MP hadn't noticed the CIO button Chips had pinned on his fez,
he might have got away with it.

Despite his two hundred and fifty pounds of
brawn, and his sea-wolf appearance, there never
was a gentler guy than Chips toward friends,
though he has a not-so-gentle record with respect
to enemies. Seattle is a place he can't go back to,
because once he was compelled to throw a Seattle
cop over a balustrade, with nothing on the other
side of it except the ground twenty feet below. And
he had his Second Mate's ticket taken away from
him ten years ago for knocking all a Shipping Commissioner's front teeth down his throat at a sign-on.
The Commissioner had called all union men the
one name seamen won't take. Also, sundry West
Coast scabs and phonies still can see the marks of
Chips's huge fists when they look in the mirror.
Once he turned a Congressional hearing into an

uproar by calling the assembled inquisitors just the kinds of sons-of-bitches they were.

It was a secret session, so Chips got no publicity. He had just been repatriated from Murmansk, where he had waited ninety days for a ship home after his double torpedoing. To pass the time he had got well acquainted around town, fighting fires every night the Nazis came over, and they came most nights. The Russians liked him, and he liked them. He got to be pals with a bunch of Russian fighter pilots, and they asked him to eat in their mess, where there was plenty of vodka. He got himself a pair of felt boots and a fur cap, and wore them around openly. He became the spokesman for several hundred American seamen who were on the beach there, after their ships had been lost. He called meetings and drafted resolutions which he then presented with great vigor to the official representatives of our government in Murmansk. The main beef of the beached hundreds was to get the hell out of there and back home where they were needed to sail ships. For all these activities, Chips was duly tagged and, when he finally got home, landed in the arms of the FBI.

"Were there any communists aboard your ship?" the agent asked him.

"What has that got to do with the convoy being knocked off?" Chips countered.

"It might have a lot to do with it," said the agent wisely.

"Well, I'll be God-damned," Chips said. "Communists would try to sink a convoy loaded with supplies for the Soviet Union! Who are we fighting anyway? Why don't you ask me if there were any fascists, any nazis, aboard my ship? I might be able to tell you something."

"I'm asking the questions," the agent said.

Then Chips was summoned to the secret Congressional hearing, where they asked him again, "Were there any communists aboard your ship?" That is when he called the Congressmen what they were.

Big as he is, Chips was the runt in his family. His father, a Newfoundlander, was six feet four and built like Chips, who is only five feet ten but weighs two-hundred and fifty pounds. Chips's father was a diver, sandhog, and deep-sea salvage-tugboat-man. As a boy he had come to New York from Newfoundland, and married a diminutive girl from what Chips called "goat-stealing Irish" stock. They had sixteen children, thirteen of them boys, including four sets of twins. Chips was one of a pair. His twin brother Piers was one of the first Canadian fliers in the last war, and was killed in France. Josh was an auto racer. He died in a crack-up on the track. Chips's Dad and his oldest brother Jack were both killed sandhogging on the construction of the Holland Tunnel in New York. A "blow" shot their huge crushed bodies through forty feet of mud and water to the surface of the Hudson. Long ago Chips lost touch with the rest of his breed, if there are any others left.

The family was living in Frisco when Chips first ran away to sea. He was thirteen then, and shipped out to China on a tramp. When he got back, he told his Dad he had decided to be a shipwright. His Dad said Dave Brown's yard in Glasgow was the best place to learn that trade, and he ought to go there right away. At fourteen, Chips worked his way to Glasgow and served a four-year apprenticeship in Dave Brown's yard, with occasional trips back to the States on freighters. On one of them, when he was seventeen, he married a little Irish girl, as his Dad had done. Nine months later she died in childbirth, Chips heard in Glasgow, but the child lived, a girl, and was brought up by her mother's people. Chips's daughter is married herself now and has a couple of kids, but Chips doesn't know where she is.

The First World War drove Chips out of the shipyard and back to sea, where he was torpedoed his first three times. When it was over, he married again in the States and made up his mind to stay ashore. His wife bore him four children in five years. She had money of her own and spent it on cars, which she loved to drive wide-open. Once they quarreled about this, and Chips enlisted in the Marines. He was in on the Haitian occupation. When he got out, he made up with his wife but took to the road. He was a boomer in the Texas and Oklahoma oilfields. He worked as a lineman on big power lines out of Reno and Las Vegas. He helped build a pipe line through to Mazatlan, Mexico. Then he drifted up to the Bakersfield oil wells in California. He was there when he heard that his wife back East and three of their four kids had been wiped out. She had bought a new steam car and opened it up on the Post Road. They had had to bury her and the three children in a single grave, they were all in so many unrecognizable pieces.

That left only Johnny, the oldest kid, who hadn't been along on the ride. Chips brought him out to the West Coast and took the boy with him on all his jobs, booming up and down the coast. Chips organized for the Wobblies, worked on dams, in boatyards as a shipwright. Johnny seemed to thrive on the life. Once Chips was sitting in his Studebaker in front of the bus station in Seattle, waiting for a guy to ride to Grant's Pass. Johnny was asleep on the back seat.

When a slight dark girl came out to catch the bus, Chips forgot all about the guy he was waiting for. She said she was going all the way to Frisco. Chips decided that was where he was going too. He needed someone to come along and take care of the kid, he said. On the way to Frisco, Chips found out the girl was only sixteen, though she looked older. She was a Syrian. But she was fed up with the Syrian idea that women had to stay at home and keep house. She wanted to be a doctor, a surgeon, but there was no way for her to get to be that, so she was going to be the closest thing she could to it, a nurse. That was why she was running away from Seattle to Frisco, to study nursing.

By the time they reached Frisco, Chips had convinced the girl that she ought to be a surgeon after all. He said he would give her the money to be it. Three days later they were married. When the girl's old man got on their trail and found them, he threatened to have Chips up for rape and violation of the Mann Act. But it blew over, and the old man got reconciled. The girl made Johnny a good mother.

For a time Chips stuck pretty close to Frisco, earning the money to put the girl through the University of California. She finished and went on to Johns Hopkins in Baltimore. For a long time they didn't see much of each other. She kept Johnny with her, and he went back to sea. Then he got into the rank-and-file movement in the old International Seamen's Union, which broke the control of the phonies. He went through the East Coast strike in '34, then the '35 tanker strike on the West Coast. After that, he shipped around the world on the Dollar Line and was gone seven months. When he got back, the girl had had enough. Even though she had modern ideas about herself, she was like other girls in one thing. She wanted her man at her side, not always everywhere else.

They loved each other, but what could they do about it? Chips had to roam. That was the way he was made. And she had to stay put, because she had to get somewhere in her profession, and because of Johnny. So they were divorced. But neither one could take it. A few months later they were remarried, and by a priest. Chips convinced her he'd always travel and she concluded she'd rather have him like he was than not at all. By this time she had finished at Johns Hopkins and gone back home to Seattle to start her practice. Chips shipped out to the East Coast and came back on the Lillian Luckenbach to strike her and start the big West Coast tie-up of 1936-37. The Embarcadero knew him on the picket line. Then he put in a spell organizing power-linemen in the oilfields. Home pulled him back to Seattle, where now they had a nice house in the country and a chicken farm. He worked in the shipyards, and his wife thought maybe he had come back for good. He tried to think so himself and built a lot of brooder houses and such in his spare time. But now when he was home, his wife was always gone—at the hospital, out on a call, at a medical lecture, or else she had people in to talk shop, medical stuff he knew nothing about. Nobody wanted to hear what he had to say, and he knew something too.

About then, Chips threw the policeman over the balustrade. He and his wife were divorced again, and Chips went back to Frisco. He was a patrol-

man for the union until the European war started
brewing in the summer of 1939. Smelling excite-
ment, Chips went east and shipped out for England. When he got there, Hitler had invaded Poland.

Every now and then he would hear from his
former wife that Johnny was doing very well in
high school and was getting ahead of his age. In
1941, Johnny entered the University of Washington on a scholarship. He was only sixteen. Not long
after Pearl Harbor, Chips got a letter saying
Johnny had run away to Vancouver and was now
out in the South Pacific on a Canadian ship. The
next letter told how Jap planes had got Johnny's
ship. The crew were all safely in the boats when
the planes came back. After the Japs finished ma-
chine-gunning the boats, there were no survivors.

The girl Chips made into a surgeon is out in the
South Pacific herself now, a major in the Army
Medical Corps. He never hears from her, now that
there is no Johnny to write about. Maybe they will
meet up out there some day, for Chips has a score
to settle with the Japs and is going back to the Pacific when the European war is finished. Then,
maybe, the two of them will find out something
about themselves which I discovered from just
knowing Chips.

Chips's fo'c'sle is the favorite hang-out of the
armored force group we are taking up to the front.
Chips shoots the breeze with them most of the night

while his room-mate, Bos'n Bruce, runs the non-stop poker game in the messroom. Chips's special pal is a very young lieutenant, immensely popular with his outfit. This boy went through plenty of hell at the Kasserine Pass, but he doesn't show it. Always kidding with the GI's in the outfit. One day he gives a burlesque military lecture on the hatch. His subject is "The 1943 Model WAC," with illusstrations on a blackboard. It is an act at a joint Army-Merchant Marine-Navy entertainment we are having to keep everybody feeling good on the way up to the front. The lieutenant's lecture, which is of the men-only variety, is the hit of the show.

All the time he's aboard, the lieutenant sleeps in Chips's fo'c'sle on the settee, instead of down in the 'tweendecks. When we get where we're going, Chips gives him everything he can think of—his rubber boots and rain gear (there aren't any more in the slop chest, so Chips will get mighty wet on deck crossing the wintry ocean back), cartons of cigarettes, tools that might come in handy on a tank, his favorite sheath knife. This young lieutenant left college to get into the war, just as Johnny did. Some of the crew kid Chips about the boy, not understanding. And they still don't understand why Chips can't keep anything but powdered milk on his stomach for days after we drop the lieutenant and the other boys at the front.

We've finished discharging and are about ready to leave port when the lieutenant shows up in a jeep. He has got back from his outfit to pay us one last visit. Chips is working on deck when the boy comes up the gangway. The way Chips looks when he sees him makes you wish to God you'd never ribbed the big guy about anything.

CHAPTER FOUR

Where I Belong

THIS IS WHERE I BELONG. Not often in a man's life does he know for sure that he is in the right place at the right time. But I have known that from the day I made up my mind to join the SS Booker T. Washington. One short talk with Captain Mulzac convinced me. I would make just one trip, I thought. Three days later I was aboard and we sailed in convoy.

Now it is almost two years later, and I am still aboard, an old-timer and no longer a first-tripper. Again we are on the way over, the fifth time for me, and a long way from any land. A gale is whistling through the slats of my black-out port and I have to brace my feet on the deck, as I type, to keep my chair from sliding with the heavy roll of the ship. Over the desk are the pictures of my wife, my three sons, my daughter. To the left hanging from the bulkhead is my life preserver, with red flashlight, knife, and whistle attached by a lanyard. Beside it is the abandon-ship kit for my lifeboat, containing morphine, sulfa, burn ointment, and dressings.

Many things acted together to bring me here to this small cabin on the boat deck of the SS Booker T. Washington, where I have known a contentment more complete and steady than I have ever before experienced. Chance played no part in bringing me here, however, nor did external compulsion. I was thirty-nine when I joined up, and over the draft age. I had a good job in New York. My family needed me at home. For all that, I couldn't stay off this ship. My being here is inevitable, the reasons for it going back through my whole life and the lives of my forefathers, back as far as another John Beecher, who came to America from England in 1637.

That John Beecher was no different from the millions of immigrants who came on the later tides, just a working stiff looking for a chance. First he tried the Massachusetts Bay Colony, but the next year he joined some guys who wanted to start a brand-new one. They went on to Connecticut, where they built a blockhouse and some log cabins which they named New Haven. Seven men stayed on through the first winter to keep the Indians off, while the rest went back to Massachusetts Bay. John Beecher was one of the seven who stayed. When spring came, he was dead. Whether the Indians got him, or just the cold and hunger, the record doesn't tell. He left a widow in Massachusetts Bay, with a little boy. She wanted to go back to England, where she had kinsfolk, but the others persuaded her to come on to Connecticut with them. She was a midwife. They would need a midwife in New Haven, to get all the children safely born— the children they had to have to make their idea of a town come true. She went with them, and her little boy grew up to be the town blacksmith. He made the saws and hammers to build houses, the nails to hold them together, the plows to break the ground.

The Beechers were still the blacksmiths in New Haven at the time of the American Revolution. The one my oldest boy is named for made guns for Washington's soldiers. He had a son, Lyman, who finished Yale in 1797 and became a preacher. In the eighteen-thirties, Lyman went West to Cincinnati and opened up Lane Theological Seminary, which became a seed-bed of the Abolitionist movement. Lyman's oldest son, my great-grandfather Edward, went further west to Illinois. He was one of a group of young fellows who left Yale to start colleges in the new states that had none. They called themselves "the Yale Band." Edward was

the first President of the first college in Illinois.
Along with his friend Elijah Lovejoy, he founded
the Illinois Anti-Slavery Society in 1837. He just
missed being with Lovejoy in the Alton riot,
when the slavery men lynched Lovejoy and
smashed the presses on which he'd been printing
the truth about them. It's a landmark in the history
books now, though at the time my great-grandfather's story of Lovejoy's lynching was stolen from
the United States mails on its way to the eastern
newspapers. He had to rewrite it and send it
through another way, and it was the first account
to be printed. The end of slavery looked a long way
off then, except to people like Elijah Lovejoy and
my great-grandfather.

Another one of Lyman's children was Harriet
Beecher Stowe, who wrote "Uncle Tom's Cabin"
out of what she saw and heard at Lane Seminary.
Still another was Henry Ward Beecher, the anti-
slavery orator. My grandfather was a preacher in
upstate New York who married a clipper-ship captain's daughter from Newburyport, Massachusetts.
Edward Everett Hale, who wrote "The Man Without a Country," was a cousin of hers. My father took
after the blacksmiths rather than the preachers and
writers in the family, and went to work in a Chicago steel mill when he finished college. My mother
was a teacher at Northwestern University. Her
father was an Irish immigrant coal miner, a member of the Knights of Labor. According to family

gossip, he had been one of the "Molly McGuires" in Pennsylvania back in the days when terrorism was the only defense the miners had against their bosses.

My father rose fast in the steel business and had become a top official with offices in New York when I was born in 1904. But the panic of 1907 transplanted his company's headquarters to Birmingham, Alabama, where I was brought up. All told, I have spent twenty eight of my forty one years in the South. I lived and worked, or went to school, in Alabama, Georgia, Mississippi, Florida, North Carolina, and Virginia. I also lived and worked, or went to school, in New York, New Jersey, Massachusetts, New Hampshire, Vermont, Indiana, and Wisconsin. I have been in every one of the forty-eight states, most of them repeatedly. So when people ask me what part of the country I am from, I am at a real loss to answer them, for I don't feel that I belong to any one part, but to all of it. From what I have seen, America is all one country, and what its various regions have in common is far more considerable than what divides them. Those who harp on regional differences and seek to preserve them—even to exalt them above the democratic traditions of the whole nation—are bad Americans. They will be remembered as Lovejoy's lynchers are remembered, and their defeat is just as certain.

We lived on the top of a hill in Birmingham,

with woods all around and houses far apart, surrounded by gardens. Down in the valley on one side was Smithfield, close-ranked Negro shacks fronting on muddy unpaved streets and garbage-littered alleys. Here the "honey-wagons" used to go, collecting the accumulation from thousands of privies. In the valley behind our house were blast furnaces and beehive coke ovens, surrounded by more rows of Negro shacks. Along both banks of Village Creek in that valley the privies stretched in unbroken lines, emptying into the water where Negro children swam and caught crawfish. Yet when I was small, I was not conscious that any gulf separated me from these dark-skinned children.

Sara, our cook, had a little girl about my age whom she brought to work with her. Her name was Corinne and she was my favorite playmate, because she liked to make up imaginary countries too and draw boundaries, build cities and lay out railroads all over our acre lot. The white kids in the neighborhood thought that was foolish and played Civil War all the time. When I played with them, they made me be the Yankee army all by myself, which wasn't much fun for me. So I played with Corinne all one summer until the neighbors did some talking to our housekeeper (my mother was away), and she told Sara she couldn't bring Corinne to work with her any more.

I remember one Fourth of July I came into the kitchen waving a big American flag. "Salute this flag!" I commanded Sara, "It made you free!" But Sara made like she hadn't heard me and went on pouring batter into the corn-stick irons. I couldn't understand why Sara was so unpatriotic, and I was a whole lot older before I did.

After Corinne was chased off, Rob was my playmate. He was our gardener, the younger brother of Colonel T. O.'s coachman, Tom, in the next block. Rob was a beautiful young Negro, very slim, yet immensely strong. He would hold his arm straight out and let me chin myself on it, like a bar, as many times as I was able. He knew all kinds of stories, Br'er Rabbit stories and blast furnace stories and coke oven stories. He told me about the coal mines where they worked Negro convicts and how the trusty would come through the stockade before dawn singing, "Wake up, mens, and git yo' fo' o'clock coffee!" Bammity, bam, bam, the hobnails would hit the floor as the convicts piled out of their straw bunks, and the chains clanked on their legs. By five o'clock, they were at work down in the mine, and they didn't get back on top until after seven in the evening. All those who failed to dig their "tasks" each day, even if it was because they were sick, were one after another stripped down to their waists and tied to a post in the center of the stockade. Then they were lashed till the blood ran down their backs. Rob was only seventeen, but he knew a lot about the convict mines. I never asked him where he learned it.

All day Rob would ride me around on his wheelbarrow, telling me stories. I would ride out on the load of rocks and weeds he was dumping in the woods, then back in again on the leaf mold he had scooped up to enrich our hilltop. He believed in my imaginary countries, too, and about the Purps. The Purps were the aboriginal inhabitants of my hilltop continent. I called them Purps because they had purple skins. Rob felt very sympathetic toward the Purps. I had a guilty feeling about my race, of which I was the President and Emperor, having run the Purps out, so I established a reservation for them, on that far corner of the lot where we kept the manure pile and the logs for the fireplaces. Later on when I was in school, I wrote a History of the Purps—a kind of decline and fall it was— and invented a Purpic language, with a grammar and exercises.

Rob was the most beautiful whistler I ever heard. His whistling would wake me up each summer morning at six, when he started work, blending with that of the mockingbirds in our trees. He whistled mostly blues, and sometimes he would sing a verse in between. Rob was cakewalk champion of Smithfield, too. Strong as he was, Rob had very slender wrists and hands like a pianist's. My father soon found out that Rob could do anything with those hands. We never had to call in a carpenter, plumber, or electrician. Whatever was wrong, Rob learned how to fix it, though his main job was being the gardener. Anything and everything would grow for him. He turned that rocky hilltop of ours into something so lovely it hurts me to remember, the look of it in the spring sun and the smells on the soft air with the green grass so cool under the bare soles of my feet. Such roses as we had, pansies and iris and sweet peas and asters, lavender wistaria climbing up the trees and porches, honeysuckle on the rock walls Rob's hands had build. From spring to fall our vegetables came from his garden—asparagus, green peas, tomatoes, beets, radishes, green onions, new potatoes.

We had one of the first automobiles in town. It was a huge steam car, very complex and dangerous to operate. Rob learned to drive it in no time. It kept breaking down, but he could always fix it. When it caught fire from itself in the garage, Rob put the fire out with his bare hands, burning them so badly that he had to be sent to the hospital. In the years Rob stayed with us, he taught himself to become an expert automobile mechanic. We never had to send a car to the shop for repairs or even for general overhauling. Rob did it all. He also became a competent house-painter—inside and out— paper-hanger, plasterer, carpenter, plumber, and electrician. When he decided to leave us and go in business for himself, my father lent him the money to buy a truck. It was a pity for him to waste all his talents on us. But Rob hadn't been long on his own before some white men called on him and told him

he had to join the colored auxiliary of their union.
That meant he would pay them dues but have no
vote or any say at all in union affairs. That also
meant he would get only odds and ends of jobs,
away out in the county, just what was left over after
the white union members had taken their pick. Rob
told the men he would think it over. A few days
later while he was at work plastering inside a house
the white men took out the spark plugs of his truck
parked on the street in front. After pouring sand
in all the cylinders, they screwed the spark plugs
back in. When Rob came out and started his engine, the sand scored the insides of all the cylinders,
ruining the whole block. He didn't wait for what
they would do to him next, but came back to work
for us.

Rob hated the shack where he lived on a muddy
Smithfield street you couldn't even drive over in a
car. He bought a lot out in the country, in a settle-
ment of Negroes who wanted something better, and
built his own house from the ground up, doing all
the work himself in his spare time. He and his wife
had one boy, who was one of the first graduates of
the Negro high school which the Ku Klux Klan
threatened to burn down when it was built. Rob
sent his boy to Tuskegee Institute and the boy went
North after graduation to become a prosperous
plumber. The last time I saw him, Rob was getting
old and sad. I hardly knew him for the early morning whistler who used to ride me on his wheel-

barrow to the woods and who alone could join me
in my imaginary world where only the Purps were
wronged because of the color of their skins.

There was no school for the colored children
around the blast furnaces and coke ovens in the valley behind our hilltop. They had to climb over our
hill to go to school on the other side, in Smithfield.
Usually they would come over and go home again
in a body, for protection. They would pass right by
our gate and many's the time I saw them running
to or from school, in a hail of rocks, with the tough
white boys from my school chasing them. Raymond
was the toughest. Once Raymond just walked up to
a colored boy on the street. When he got right on
him, Raymond drew back and threw a huge rock
he had behind his back. It knocked a hole in the
colored boy's forehead. I know, because I saw it.
I kept thinking our principal would do something
to Raymond, but he didn't. Nothing happened to
Raymond until many years later when another
Klansman slipped up behind Raymond with an
automobile crank and knocked a hole in his head
too.

Stank and Jimbo and that boy who lived next the
Confederate graveyard and always carried brass
knucks in his hip pocket would hide in the bushes
along the path by the graveyard after school. Nobody took care of the graves any more and the place
was just like a jungle in there. And when a colored
girl came by on the way home from school, Stank

and Jimbo and the boy with the brass knucks would jump out and drag her inside the graveyard.

At big recess we would watch the chain gang while we ate our lunches. They were building a street along the far edge of the schoolyard so Judge Maxwell could get in and out with his Cadillac. They were all Negroes. They all wore black and white suits plastered with red mud. They all had chains from ankle to ankle so they could only take short steps and couldn't run. They worked under the gun, the white guard always standing with his rifle slanted in their direction. He also had a big pistol in a holster, and a belt full of cartridges. I don't remember ever hearing that chain gang sing while they worked on the street, and when they got their dinner—tin plates full of cowpeas out of a black iron washpot with a fire under it—they just ate the cowpeas without any sound but the sound of their eating. Then, one day out in the woods behind the school, I found a leg chain along the path, where some Negro had somehow managed to escape and file off his chain. I took that leg chain home inside my coat, not telling anybody about it, and I locked it in my box I had a key to, along with some old lead bullets my grandfather said came from Gettysburg battlefield. . . .

1920

The street was straight and narrow up to the steel plant. The buildings along it were low and dirty—

pawnshops, cheap cafes, stores selling overalls, work shoes, canvas gloves with red stars on the gauntlets. In the pawnshop windows were gold watches and pistols. The loan sharks took these in for security, and when they couldn't get security they lent money without it: they knew how to collect. Two bits on the dollar every pay day was the interest rate—about ten per cent a week. I knew a Negro up in the plant who had borrowed $10, paid back $60 and still owed $25. On pay day the loan sharks stood out in front of their shops under the three gold balls and collared the men who owed them money as they came from the paycar at the head of the street. The cops walked up and down. All the beggars were there—the old colored man with the guitar on his leg stumps, and the little boy holding out a cup, the old colored woman who read a braille Bible out loud. The snake oil man stood on his wagon and spieled. A dollar a bottle the snake oil was, and it would cure lost manhood, lumbago, "bad blood" (syphilis), or anything else that ailed you.

As you went up the street into the steel plant, the blast furnaces were on the right; the open hearth, Bessemer converters, soaking pits, and rolling mills on the left. I went to the left, to the open hearth. I was sixteen and had a good job, keeping track of everything that happened on the open hearth and up at the Bessemer converters: how much pig iron they had in the mixers from hour to hour; how many pots the converters blew; when No. 6 furnace charged scrap, melted down, took hot metal, was all-in, tapped, what she made—whether rail, plow, wire, or structural steel; how long the helpers made bottom on No. 3; when No. 9 went down for repairs to the front-wall and when they switched the flame back on her. All this meant I had to be on the go from when I started at seven in the morning till I got off at five-thirty in the evening. Later I was on nights, from five-thirty in the evening till six-thirty in the morning.

But I was lucky because I had a chance to learn everything. I would skip college, I decided. When I was eighteen, I would go to work as a third-helper on a furnace, and after a couple or three years of that get to be a pit boss, then night superintendent, and so on up. That's what I thought until some things began to bother me.

At first I didn't know what it was bothering me. I'd been living in the South a long time. Wherever you live, you get used to things, how they are, as if they had to be that way. Then something happens. One day you come to. You suddenly see the things you've just been looking at.

It hit me one Saturday night when we'd tapped out all the heats early. It was about three o'clock in the morning and I could have gone home and got some night-time sleep for a change. Instead I went into the mill office, grabbed a sheaf of yellow paper, and started to write. I didn't know what: there

was just something that had to get said. Four
or five hours later I had used up all the yellow
paper and went home to bed in Sunday morning
sunlight. These are the things that had been bothering me:

Up and down the open hearth floor you saw only
white men: old melters with their hairy chests and
bellies, helpers shoveling in the furnace glow,
charging car men riding their huge machines,
cranemen in their high cages, pull-ups at their
levers, dinky engineers with pots of sloshing red
metal from the Bessemers. White men only on the
tapping platform when a furnace went over, the
dazzling steel cataracting in the ladle. White men
in the pulpit where the Bessemers were controlled,
the great flames licking into billowing orange fume
beyond the window. White men on the pouring
tables where they teemed the steel in molds—the
steel pourer at the lever next the smoking ladle, the
tableman spooning out a test from the liquid metal
column, the ingot chaser with his record pad, the
ladle craneman in his dark cage where the switches
crackled blue, the test boy crawling out of the aluminum box where he'd been asleep. All white.

All Negroes though on the slaghole gang. After
the steel ran blinding into the ladle came the slag,
softer on the eyes, pink through blue furnace glasses,
sudsy, spilling over the ladle sides and swirling
down the runners into slagpots. When the crane
picked the ladle up to swing it over to the pouring

table, the Negroes on the slaghole gang came swarming out of the tunnels underneath the furnaces, turned hoses on the foamy slag clotting the pit's dirt floor, then hit it with picks and shovels while it was still red. They said no white man could keep up with that gang. As they worked next the slagpots, little volcanoes built up as the stuff crusted over and the molten inside kept erupting through. Sometimes one of these would blow like a big Roman candle, and the slaghole gang would duck back into the tunnels fast as cockroaches, then come on back and hit it again with their picks and shovels. Sometimes, too, a slagpot would blow all the way up and kill people. The trouble with a slag burn was the phosphorus in the stuff: it not only burned; it poisoned. A slag burn no bigger than a match head would spread into a pus-filled sore the size of a quarter.

Negroes worked with the brickmasons repairing and rebuilding furnaces and pulling out checker chambers. They didn't lay brick. Never. Before a furnace had time to cool down even, they went in with picks and sledges and started knocking out the old steel-bitten, slag-crusted brickwork. That was their part of the job, that and wheeling in new brick when the masons got to working. They piled the old débris and new brick out in front of the open hearth floor, and it was their lookout for cranes with loads, charging cars, and dinkies pulling hot metal pots.

Down at the lime plant which burnt limestone and dolomite for the open hearth, white men were the burners and the cranemen, Negroes the sweepers. That was the worst place to work in the whole steel plant. Lime or dolomite dust in your shoes will raise big blisters on your sweaty feet, will raise welts on your eyeballs, burning as the moisture slakes it. It does worse things when you breathe it. At the lime plant everything was covered with the deadly white dust—from the floor under the big rotary kilns up to the tops of the tall stacks pluming dusty smoke. Men who worked there were powdered with dust from head to foot. The Negroes would have to go under the kilns and sweep up the dust, bending over double. You couldn't see the men under there—just the huge dust cloud they were raising. A sweeper would tie a handkerchief over his mouth and go down. He would stay five minutes and then come running out, his clothes sopped with wet, coughing. He would go drink water and hang over a rail, breathing outside air. Five minutes sweeping. Five minutes resting. That was the way they worked. A good sweeper's lungs lasted ten years on the average.

What I wrote that night was about one of those Negro sweepers, one whose lungs had given out. The company let him come to work and just lie around on a wheelbarrow waiting to die. "The company's mighty good to me," he would tell you. I wrote the piece because I had to write it—and I filled in some about his life in the company quarters across the mill fence, about how he got in the hands of a loan shark, things like that. A lot of people read that piece then, though it hasn't been printed till now. One was a great poet. He said, "You have got to watch out for taking sides. A writer can't afford to." I didn't know what he meant then, because I didn't know about any sides. I had just put it down the way it was.

1934

The county doctor really put the neoarsephena- mine to them. Every Thursday the truck from the Negro prison farm would unload at the courthouse, and the syphilitics—men and women—would be marched into the gloomy basement under the guards' guns. There they would sit on benches along with the Negro relief clients waiting for their shots. The country doctor came from what is called one of the best families in South Carolina and was just doing this as part of his training, not because he had any love for it. He yanked the Negroes around, yelled at them, jabbed the needle into them as if it were a bayonet. When a woman had a reaction and keeled over on the stone floor foaming at the mouth, it didn't bother the doctor any. He just let her lie.

When I first came to that city as relief administra- tor, I was warned not to call any of the Negro case workers Miss or Mrs. My predecessor had slipped up once and said "Miss Appleby" instead of "Victoria" when speaking to a Negro case worker. Somebody had overheard and a delegation went to the state capital about it. When I arrived to take over the job, the chairman of my advisory committee said he was glad I was raised in Alabama: they knew how to handle Negroes in Alabama, he said.

Victoria Appleby was the best social worker I ever knew. There was an uproar when I raised her pay from $19.62 to $23.08 a week. This was more than a lot of white people in the organization were getting. They came to see me about it, and they weren't satisfied when I explained that it was because Victoria Appleby had professional training which they didn't have. What difference did that make, they wanted to know—wasn't she colored and weren't they white? The county doctor didn't like my raising her pay either and took it out on her relief clients. He refused to certify the transfer of a seriously arthritic relief worker from a swamp drainage project to a job where he wouldn't have to work in water up to his hips. When Victoria Appleby went to him about it, just as nicely as she knew how, he cursed her for "an uppity black bitch" and drove her out of the clinic. As I have said, he came from what is called one of the best families in South Carolina.

One day a delegation of important business men called at my office. They said the strawberries were rotting in the fields in adjoining counties because the lazy city Negroes wouldn't go out and pick them. They demanded I cut off all Negro relief in the city. I said I couldn't without finding out how many workers were needed, what they got paid for picking berries, and what the living conditions were. The delegation said if I wouldn't come along on the proposition they would see to it that I got my orders. Before the day was over a telegram from the state administrator ordered me to stop all direct and work relief to Negroes until further notice. Relief to whites was to continue.

I sent three investigators into the strawberry fields. They found pickers were clearing—over what they were charged for food and lodging— from 20 cents to a dollar a week. Sixty men, women, and children lived in a barn, sleeping on the floor. Twenty were bunked in a one-room shack. For water they walked a mile or so to the branch. For privy they used the woods. The local newspapers wouldn't touch the story, but when I got a progressive outside newspaper to send in a reporter and his stories began running, the state administrator asked me to investigate.

1943

It was New Year's Day and I had to make a speech in Bridgeport, Connecticut, not far from where the first John Beecher settled in 1638, looking for a chance, but found death instead. The place was a Negro church and my audience were all Negroes. The occasion was not only New Year's

Day but the 80th anniversary of Lincoln's Emancipation Proclamation. I had been asked to speak because I was the regional director of the President's Committee on Fair Employment Practice for New York and New England. This was an agency set up by President Roosevelt to carry out his order that all Americans—regardless of race, creed, color or national origin—should have a fair chance to work at their highest level of skill in war industries. Before coming to the Northeastern region, I had represented the FEPC in the South.

What I had to say that night took the form of a poem when I wrote it out beforehand. It gives all the rest of the reasons which brought me up the gangway of the SS Booker T. Washington a few months later, to serve under a Negro captain. So I am making it the next chapter of this book.

CHAPTER FIVE

After Eighty Years

I

Lincoln was pushed into it
they are still telling us
yes
after eighty years
they are still handing us that

I'd put it this way
Lincoln was just slow to catch on
slow to take hold
like many another man
trusting the experts but not himself fully
not really believing
in what he was fighting for
because he hadn't made his own mind up

Once Lincoln made his mind up
and wrote:
"thenceforward and forever free"
he started being the Lincoln we remember
and the war for Union
turned into a people's war
that could not be lost

Emancipation
kept England off the South's side
because the English working people
could not be made to fight for slavery

Emancipation
brought the Negroes in on the North's side
and turned the scale
Lincoln said so then
but after eighty years our school history books
still have nothing to say
about the 200,000 Negro soldiers and sailors
who lost a third of their number
fighting for their freedom and the Union
while the South warned
"none will be taken prisoners."
A Memphis slavedealer turned general
Nathan Bedford Forrest
captured Fort Pillow on the Mississippi
having ten men to the Union's one
and three under the white flags of surrender
bayoneted to death or buried alive
the Negro wounded
penned the Negro prisoners in wooden buildings
then burned them down.
It was another story
at Port Hudson, Ship Island, Fort Wagner and
*   Nashville*
where Negroes fought on even terms
and it was a far different story

that day in 1865
when black cavalry rode into Richmond
at the head of Grant's army.
Behind these black fighters
were black workers for freedom
in hundreds of thousands
on the docks where munitions were unloaded
on Union fortifications from the Red River to the
        James and Potomac
builders teamsters cooks and nurses of the wounded
while by the hundreds of thousands
Negroes left their plows in the fields of slavery
seeking refuge in the camps of the blue armies
seeking work in freed fields
then having found it
they plowed to feed and clothe blue armies
while gray armies
went bare and hungry
After eighty years
we ought to know these things
better than we do

II

Eighty years
are a long while to be waiting
for somebody to finish
what Lincoln began.

Starting in 1863
Negro Americans with their own blood and toil

have bought and paid for freedom
full and unconditional
ten times over
and now in 1943
Negro Americans
in the army and the navy
by the hundreds of thousands
are fighting for the world's freedom
as well as their own . . .

In Lowndes County Alabama
Negroes are more than 85 per cent of all the people
but in all that county
not one Negro votes
not one Negro is called Mister by white people
and the few Negroes who own land
don't dare build themselves decent homes
for fear the white folks would resent it.
I saw a tumbledown tenant cabin in Lowndes
from which three dark boys had gone North
two of them are college deans now and the third
      a scientist.

A few years back
the sharecroppers down in Lowndes tried to
      organize
because somebody from the outside
came in and told them
the President of the United States said they had a
      right to.

They counted the bodies they found afterward
the ones shot on dry land
and the ones that washed up bound hand and foot
on the Alabama River bank
but there were plenty still missing.
One planter told me
he'd been merciful himself
he just called a meeting of his croppers
in the church
and publicly whipped
the two or three that got mixed up in the union
that taught the rest of them a lesson
he told me

Between 1935 and 1940
400,000 farms were wiped off the southern map
400,000 families had to pull up stakes
more than 2,000,000 people cut adrift,
You've heard about the white farmers
from Oklahoma, Texas and Arkansas
and who went to California
and maybe you saw "The Grapes of Wrath"
but did you know
40,000 families were tractored out in Alabama
mostly Negroes
more people than lost out in Oklahoma?

No
we don't hear about them
nor about the 35,000 families in Georgia

who lost their chance to make a crop
they were mostly Negroes too

Where they all went
nobody exactly knows
some lived on where they were
in their little shacks and cabins
catching what wagehand work there was
sixty cents a day from can till can't
or picking cotton at 75c a hundred
some moved to town and went on relief
some hit the migrant trails
from Louisiana up through Arkansas and Kentucky
        on into Michigan
from Florida on up the coast to Lake Ontario and
        Maine

I got to know these people
down in Florida
and I would like to say something about them

They were living on the canal banks
in stinking quarters and barracks
sometimes thirteen people in a room
or in tarpaper huts and shelters in the weeds
and every morning before dawn came
they climbed on to trucks in the quarters
bound for the beanfields
where all day
everybody that could pick

down to the five and six year olds
picked
kneeling in the black Everglades muck.
It would be dark night again
when they got back to quarters
and all night long
the jook joints stayed open
so whiskey dice and women
could eat up the earnings of the day

That was the white growers' idea
of how to hold labor —
keep the Negroes broke
they said
and instead of a church or a school
a grower would build a jook joint
at the center of his quarters
to get back at night
what he paid out in the day

When the government came in
and started building a model camp for the Negroes
with screened shelters and shower baths
        and flush toilets
an infirmary a community center a school and
        playgrounds
laundry tubs and electric irons
the growers raised hell
what was the government's idea anyway
ruining the rental value of their canal bank
        quarters

*and fixing to ruin their labor with a lot of useless
        luxury
besides the Negroes wouldn't use the camp
they liked to be dirty
they liked to be diseased
they liked to be vicious*

*When the growers saw
the government was going ahead anyway
they said
"You will have to hire a bunch of camp guards
white men
and have them patrol the camp
with clubs and pistols
or the Negroes
won't pay the rent
they will stop working entirely
and they will take the camp to pieces"*

*Let me tell you what happened
I know
because I was there
and I was in charge of the camp*

*When the day came to open
we just opened the gate
and let anybody in that wanted to come in
no hand-picking no refenrences or anything like
        that
it was enough for us*

that a family wanted to live there
and not on the canal bank

We didn't hire any white guards either
and nobody carried a club or a pistol
in all that camp that held a thousand people

We just got them altogether in the community
center
and told them it was their camp
and they could make it a bad camp
or they could make it a good camp
that was up to them
and there wouldn't be any laws or ordinances
except the ones they made for themselves
through their elected council

Then for a week
they had a campaign in camp
with people running for office the first time in their
lives
and after the campaign
people voted for the people they wanted to repre-
sent them
for the first time in their lives
and after it was over
they celebrated with a big dance in the community
center
and nobody got drunk and disorderly
and nobody cut anybody with a knife
and the only reason was

they had themselves a Council ...
after that
the Council made the laws and ordinances
Council said
nobody's dog could run around loose
he had to be tied up
Council said
a man couldn't beat his wife up in camp
and when a man came in drunk one night and did
he was out of camp by morning
Council said
people had to pay their rent
because out of that rent money
came camp baseball equipment
and it kept up the nursery school
so when people wouldn't pay
Council put them out ...
finally Council said
it's a long way to any store
we ought to have our own store
and that's how the co-op started
without a dollar in it
the people didn't put up ...

Some of the men and women on that Council
couldn't so much as write their names
remember these were just country Negroes
off sharecrop farms in Georgia and Alabama
just common ordinary cottonpickers
the kind

Lowndes County planters say
would ruin the country
if they had the vote . . .

All I know is
my eyes have seen
democracy work

III

Freedom
is a whole lot more
than just not being owned by somebody.
Lincoln knew that.

Freedom starts with not being owned
but it also means
having a say in how you are governed
a home you can call yours
land if you're a farmer
that you can stay on year after year
hold it and improve it and get the benefit of it
either working for yourself alone
or a lot of farmers altogether working one big farm
for the good of all
and freedom means if you're a worker
the chance to learn the job of your choice
and the right to work at that job

Now
the United States government is putting up hun-
      dreds of millions of dollars

to teach new trades to citizens
both men and women
so they can build the planes the tanks the ships and
        guns
we must have to win
I was down in Georgia
looking over this government training program
and I saw fine new shops
full of the most uptodate machinery
millions of dollars worth
and I saw where thousands of white people
men and women
were being taught at the expense of the government
how to weld ships and rivet airplanes and the rest
but I didn't see any Negroes in the shops
though Negroes are more than one out of every
        three
of Georgia's people
so I asked where were they . . .
this was kind of embarrassing to the authorities
they admitted they weren't training many
and said the reason was
the Negroes couldn't get jobs
even if they were trained
so there wasn't any use training them . . .

I had to go a long way in Georgia
to find any Negroes getting training
and when I found them
this is what I saw . . .

bare classrooms with benches and blackboards
not a lathe nor a drill press nor a welding machine
         in the place
men trying to learn through their eyes
what could only be learned through their hands

In all of Georgia
not one Negro woman
was getting even this kind of training
and when I asked why not
the authorities said to me surprised
"If Negro women could get war jobs
what would people do for cooks?"

Then there were the Negro carpenters
I talked to in Houston, Texas
two hundred of them in Houston
men who had been carpenters all their lives
and the white carpenters wouldn't let them in the
         union
and that meant they couldn't even work
on the Negro housing project
or on any kind of war building that was going on
and since there wasn't anything else left to work on
they were getting desperate . . .

There was a Negro welding class in Houston
just like the white classes
the whites got jobs welding in the shipyards
the day they finished their course

but the Negro welders
are working at common labor
or at nothing . . .

So it goes
all over the South
in munitions at Memphis
aircraft at Dallas and Nashville
at the Macon arsenal and Pascagoula shipyard
no skilled jobs for Negroes
and in many places
no unskilled ones either . . .
just whatever happens to be left over
when the white people are used up
or whatever work is too heavy or nasty
for white people to do
is what the Negroes get . . .
that's the way it still is
after eighty years

IV

"Thenceforward and forever free"
were Lincoln's words
but he didn't stop there
no
he said more:
"and the Executive government of the United
        States,
including the military and naval authority thereof,

will recognize and maintain the freedom of such
            persons,
and will do no act or acts to repress such persons,
or any of them, in any efforts they may make for
            their
actual freedom."

Isn't it about time after eighty years
to make good on this
and to make good on
the Thirteenth Fourteenth and Fifteenth Amend-
            ments
to the Constitution of the United States?

I know there's a war on
but what is this war about anyway
how can we believe
how can the world's people believe
we mean to spread the light of freedom to the
            world's four corners
when there is such darkness
in America's own house?

Soon
it will be too late

CHAPTER SIX

The Skipper

THE WAITING-ROOM of the Richmond bus station is full of people, but Captain Mulzac and I find two seats together and sit down to read, since we have hours to wait for the 1 A.M. Norfolk bus. Our ship is sailing from there early in the morning, and we are on our way back from short leaves in New York. The Captain is reading a magazine review of Wendell Willkie's "One World." He reads a passage aloud to me, and we get into a discussion. The Captain thinks Willkie is one of those rare men who can go on learning all his life.

While we are talking, I glance up and notice that all the people around us have stopped what they were doing to stare at us. Gradually the whole waiting-room full of people is one great silent stare. The Captain always gets some attention because of his four gold stripes and the "scrambled eggs" on his cap visor, but this is different. I begin to tighten up inside. The Captain must notice the staring, too, but he gives no sign, and goes on talking about

Wendell Willkie's four-square stand for world-wide racial democracy.

A policeman comes in through the street door. A man just inside points to the Captain and me. The policeman comes over to us. We go on talking, and pay no attention to him standing there. The policeman then leans down to me and asks, "Is he colored?" He jerks his thumb at the Captain on the bench beside me.

"He's an American," I say.

"But isn't he colored?" the cop says belligerently.

"He's the Captain of an American ship," I say, "with one of the finest records in this war. What has whether he's colored or not got to do with anything?"

"This is Virginia," the cop says. "Can't no colored man, I don't care who he is, sit in a white folks' waiting-room in this state."

"He has taken thousands of white soldiers across the ocean on his ship, and risked his life delivering the bombs and other material they need to fight with, but he isn't good enough to sit here?"

"I got my orders to put him out."

"Then you'll have to put me out, too," I say.

The Captain has been quietly listening. "I'll go," he says. "We've got to take the ship out at six o'clock in the morning and we won't be able to if we're in a Richmond jail. But listen," and he raises his voice so all the staring people can hear. "Your orders are no good. Your orders are the kind they give in

Hitler's Germany. While we're out there fighting fascism, you fellows down here are working for fascism in the United States. After we get through smashing fascism over there, we're coming back here—right here to Virginia—and finish the job."

Nobody says anything, the whole waiting-room of white people having listened to what the Captain has said, and thinking about it. There isn't so much as a hostile look.

"I can't help it," the cop mumbles finally. "I got my orders."

The Captain and I go outside and wait for the Norfolk bus. We stand up out there for two hours, but it doesn't seem so long because of all the people —colored people—who come out of the night to shake the Captain's hand. It looks as if all of Negro Richmond has heard about Captain Mulzac's being thrown out of the bus station, and has come to pay him homage.

When the bus comes, the Captain and I go on through to the colored section in the back, where we sit down together. I expect to be the one who is asked to move this time, but the bus driver takes up my ticket and says nothing. Then we are speeding down the lonely highway along the James. I doze off and wake up as we are pulling out of Williamsburg. At Jamestown, just a few miles from here, a Dutch ship arrived in 1619, bringing 20 Negro slaves, and the thing was first started that still dishonors America. I can't sleep the rest of the way, for thinking about it. When the Captain and I go aboard the SS Booker T. Washington in the dawn light, it is like coming home from an alien land. Half an hour later, we cast off. The Captain is up on the bridge, giving the orders to the helmsman. He can maneuver a ship out of a tight spot into the stream with fewer bells than anybody the engineers ever sailed under. "Hard right . . . half ahead . . . half astern . . . hard left. . . ." Quiet and sure the commands follow each other and the ship responds, finding her way through the harbor obstructions. "Full speed ahead!" comes at last. We are on our course for the open sea and "Steady she goes!" is the master's order. "Steady she goes!" the man at the wheel repeats.

Where Hugh Mulzac was brought up, on St. Vincent's Island in the British West Indies, there were class but not racial lines. His father was a white man but his mother was "black as Mrs. Bethune," he says. They belonged to the island aristocracy. Nearby Union Island in the Grenadines with its cotton plantations belonged to them, inherited from Hugh's grandfather, an Aberdeen Scotchman who had come out as a pioneer. Hugh's father maintained a whale fishery, and a shipyard where he built schooners and whaleboats. The Mulzacs had two homes, one on St. Vincent's and another on Union Island, where they lived after school was out in the summertime. Hugh was the eldest of his mother's nine children and "the pet of the old lady." The daughter of an Episcopalian minister, she was the church organist. Hugh was a choir boy. After he finished the island school, he worked in his father's shipyard along with his brother Lamie, who is now a first-class carpenter in the Brooklyn Navy Yard.

Hugh first went to sea on one of his father's schooners, the Sunbeam, plying among the many islands which arch across the entrance to the Caribbean. A brother by his father's first wife was the Sunbeam's skipper. Though his father was determined that Hugh should study engineering in Trinidad, the boy yearned to visit the great world beyond the islands. He got his chance in Barbados. His brother, the Sunbeam's skipper, was ashore on ship's business when Captain Grandison of the Aeolus, a Norwegian barque in the harbor, sent word aboard that he needed an ordinary. Hugh quickly stowed his gear in his sea-bag and reported to Captain Grandison.

"How old are you?" the Captain asked him.

"21," Hugh lied.

"Is your brother willing for you to sign on?"

"Yes," Hugh lied again. He knew his brother would never give his permission.

"All right, lad," the Norwegian master said. "You'll do."

Captain Grandison had been a missionary in his early days. He took a great interest in Hugh and gave him navigation books to study. When the

Aeolus reached her first port of call, Wilmington in North Carolina, the Captain and Hugh went ashore together on Sunday morning. They walked along the old steets bordered with crêpe myrtles and ante-bellum homes until they found the Episcopalian church. But Hugh was stopped at the door.

"I couldn't understand," he says. "I thought I must have done something wrong. Then the man at the door said, 'We don't allow any niggers in this church.' That was the first time in my life I had heard the word 'nigger.' I just never had run into anything like that. Captain Grandison told the man at the church door that if I couldn't go inside, it was because Jesus Christ wasn't in there, and he wouldn't go in either. We went back aboard ship together and didn't come ashore any more in that port. I thought, 'If this is the United States, the land of freedom they talk about, I never want to come back.'"

The Aeolus sailed from Wilmington laden with rosin for England. Forty days later she docked in London, after near shipwreck in the Channel when, with Hugh at the wheel, she collided with a Russian barquentine, losing her anchor, foremast, and yard-arms. For the next three years, Hugh sailed on square-riggers to India, China, Australia, and around Cape Horn to South America. His father meanwhile had become reconciled to Hugh's becoming a sailor and, when Hugh had his required deep-sea time in, financed his course at the Swansea

Nautical College in Wales. Hugh was 25 when he stood for his second mate's ticket in 1911. The examination opened with the writing of a laudatory essay on the British Empire. Hugh didn't do so well with the essay, but he knew his seamanship, navigation, and mathematics thoroughly, and passed high, being granted a license in both sail and steam. He shipped out at once as a quartermaster on a steamship bound for Jamaica, where he got a mate's berth on a Norwegian fruit ship. But on arrival in Baltimore she tied up, and Hugh was beached in the country he had resolved never to come back to. This time, he was fated to stay, and to merge his lot with the tragic one of Negro Americans.

"I had an English mate's ticket in my hand," he says, "and I had no better sense than to walk right into the Merchants' and Miners' Line. I asked for a quartermaster's job."

"What?" they said. "We don't hire no niggers on deck."

Six years later Hugh Mulzac was still in Baltimore. A girl had held him. They had got married and there were children. He was still a seaman, taking whatever jobs America would let him have —deck jobs on schooners, working as a steward or as a cook on steamships. But when the United States entered the war against Germany in April, 1917, his hopes rose again. All the papers carried an urgent call for all men with sufficient sea experience to qualify themselves as officers. The War Shipping Board was establishing an upgrading school to rush them through. Hugh Mulzac applied at once, producing all his discharges and his British second mate's license. He was flatly rejected, on the ground that he wasn't an American citizen. He pointed out that other qualified non-citizens were receiving "red-ink licenses," good for the duration of the war. Ultimately one was issued to him, and he shipped to France as a second mate. When he got home, his final citizenship papers had come through. Again, he applied for admission to the Shipping Board School. This time he was accepted, graduating in two days with his American second mate's license. He kept shipping to France and England for a year and then went up for his chief mate's examination. You were allowed five days to write it. He finished all his questions in nine hours and passed. In 1920, he presented himself to the Merchant Marine Inspectors in Baltimore for the master's examinations. When he had completed them, the chief inspector gave out a story to the newspapers. He said that this man, the first Negro in his knowledge to sit for an ocean-going master's ticket, had passed higher than any candidate ever examined by his office.

It would have taken more than newspaper publicity to persuade the shipowners to give Captain Mulzac a vessel. He had to ship again as a chief mate. Then the fabulous Marcus Garvey hired him.

Garvey was a Negro promoter with dreams of becoming Emperor of Africa. He was later jailed as a swindler of his race, but in those years he appeared to Hugh Mulzac and other millions of Negro Americans as the Moses who would lead them out of economic bondage. Opportunities which had been opened to Negroes during the war were being rapidly withdrawn as the war production boom collapsed. The Ku Klux Klan was organizing all over the nation to drive the Negro even out of fields he had traditionally occupied. Garvey's appeal was based on the bitter disillusionment of the Negro which followed the war "to save democracy." His grandiose plan was to transport the entire American Negro population back to Africa and build a mighty black state where Negroes would rule themselves. To this end, he had acquired a vast concession in Liberia, where colonization would commence, and had founded a steamship company, the Black Star Line.

Garvey had visions of a huge future fleet of liners and, pending the establishment of service, sold thousands of Negroes tickets to Africa on an installment basis. To begin with, he had only the 1,000 ton "Yarmouth," plying between New York and the West Indies. Hugh Mulzac became her captain. Garvey later acquired the "Kanawha," a fast yacht, and the "General Goethals," a former German ship taken over by the government during the war. When a catastrophic depression struck American shipping in 1922, Captain Mulzac's "Yarmouth" was tied up. She rusted at the dock for years, and was finally sold for wharfage. Together with Chief Engineer John Garrett and Radio Operator Cecil Blackman, who had also served on Black Star Line ships, Captain Mulzac opened a nautical school in Harlem. It drew the most ambitious Negro youth, who dreamed of becoming the officers of Garvey's great African fleet. But the Black Star Line went broke a year later, and Captain Mulzac closed his school. There was no use preparing young men for jobs that America wouldn't let them hold.

He went back to sea as a steward on the Bull Line. Hoping that he might somehow win gradual advancement, he stuck to the line for years. They made him third mate and wireless operator. Sometimes he had to serve as third mate and steward combined. White men with far less experience and lower qualifications than himself were constantly advanced over his head. At last he asked the company to give him a chance as second mate. After all, he held an ocean-going master's license. It was impossible to give a Negro anything better, the company said, than third mate or steward, and many people objected even to that.

Hugh Mulzac quit, to save his self-respect. Long before, as a deck hand and then as a steward, he had learned to be an expert painter. If he could paint ships, he ought to be able to paint houses. He found that he could, well enough to support his wife and five children by it. But he drifted back to sea again in the early thirties, as a cook and steward. In 1934 and '35 he was one of the rank-and-filers who tried to transform the rotten old International Seamen's Union into a fighting organization. He had always believed strongly in trade unionism and had taken out his book in the British Marine Firemen and Sailors' Union back in 1910.

The black depression in shipping since 1922 had given the shipowners the chance to beat down seamen's wages and working conditions to an appallingly low level. Men were competing for the chance to ship as work-aways, just for their bunk and chow, plus one dollar or even one cent a month, to make it "constitutional." As a steward on the Calmar Line, Hugh Mulzac went out in the great East Coast strike of 1935-36. He was on the picket line and when Christmas came took a gang of hungry fellow-strikers home to a big turkey dinner he cooked himself. He helped found the National Maritime Union and went through the struggle when the labor spies and phonies on the shipowners' payroll tried to take over and break the union. They beat him with baseball bats, though he escaped being ambushed with pistols as Alex was, whipped to death with tire chains, or having the life stamped out of him on the pavement, as happened to some other honest NMU men at that period.

After the strike, Hugh Mulzac was blacklisted

and couldn't go back to sea for a year and a half. He switched to his other trade, house-painting. Then he signed on the President Polk, a world-cruise ship, as chief cook, staying aboard her for two years while she circled the globe again and again. When the Second World War put a stop to world cruises, he shipped as chief steward on two perilous trips to Egypt, with war materials for the hard-pressed British forces there. The Mediterranean was closed by Axis planes and subs. His ship had to sail all the way around the Cape of Good Hope and up the eastern coast of Africa to reach Egypt. Subs were thick in those waters and Nazi planes ferociously bombed Port Said while his ship was there.

America was at war when Captain Mulzac returned from his second trip to Egypt. As in 1917, there was a desperate shortage of experienced seamen for the new fleet of merchant ships which the yards were turning out at an undreamed-of pace. Again, the government frantically advertised in all the newspapers for ship's officers and for men with sufficient sea time to enter newly established officers' training schools.

Three years before, Hugh Mulzac had filed an application with the War Shipping Administration, setting forth his qualifications as a ship's officer, but he had never heard from it. He now resolved to stay ashore until he could sail in his proper capacity, as master of a vessel. He renewed his application with the WSA. He methodically went

from office to office of the steamship companies in
New York, until he had placed applications with
all of them. Then he waited while the months
dragged by.

From time to time the newspapers repeated the
WSA's appeals to qualified officers ashore, begging
them to report for sea duty. These were the days
when the Nazis and Japs were sinking our ships
faster than we could build them. Ships were actu-
ally delayed in sailing for the lack of officers. Unlicensed men—bos'ns and AB's and oilers—were
signed on as acting mates and engineers. Licensed
men sailed in capacities above their ratings. Masters were the scarcest of all. Old sea captains in
their seventies were haled from the snug harbors of
retirement and persuaded to take out vessels under
conditions far more dangerous and strenuous than
those they had coped with in their prime. But in
the midst of this manpower crisis created by a war
for the protection of our democratic rights, anti-
democratic practices condemned a man like Captain Mulzac to the beach.

Eventually, it required all the pressure that the
National Negro Congress, the National Maritime
Union, the national CIO, and the Negro press
could muster to break the chains of discrimination
which were keeping not only Captain Mulzac but
many other qualified Negro ship's officers idle on
the beach. The intervention of President Roosevelt
himself, and of his Committee on Fair Employ-

ment Practice, was finally required before the situation was resolved.

Captain Mulzac and the members of a protest committee from the National Negro Congress were received by Captain Edward Macaulay, deputy administrator of the War Shipping Administration in Washington. After studying Captain Mulzac's sheaf of licenses and discharges, he shook his head.

"There's only one explanation," Captain Macaulay said, "You have been the victim of rank discrimination. We're going to put an end to it. Within a few weeks we're launching a Liberty ship on the West Coast. Her name will be the SS Booker T. Washington. You will be her captain, provided you can round up enough qualified Negro seamen to make a crew."

"Do I have to sail with an all-Negro crew?" Captain Mulzac asked.

"Isn't that what you people want?"

"No," Captain Mulzac said. "All we want is a chance to sail in our ratings. We don't want segregation. If the Booker T. Washington is going to be a Jim Crow ship, I don't want to be master of her."

Captain Mulzac clung to his point and won the agreement of the WSA to his proposed "experiment." When the SS Booker T. Washington was commissioned at Los Angeles on October 15, 1942, most of her officers were Negroes for the reason that there were so many on the beach, and this was their first chance at a ship. Her unlicensed personnel, however, were about evenly divided between white and Negro. After the success of the SS Booker T. Washington, three other ships sailed with Negro captains and the barriers fell elsewhere, so that many Negroes are now sailing as mates, engineers, pursers and radio operators on ships where they may be the only members of their race among the officers.

No attempt has ever been made to maintain any fixed racial ratio on the SS Booker T. Washington, and the make-up of the ship's company has fluctuated from trip to trip. In the latest group, all the races of mankind are represented—25 are Caucasian, 17 Negro, 2 Malaysian, 1 Mongolian and 1 American Indian. The native-born whites come from Georgia, New York, California, Pennsylvania, Illinois, Ohio, Puerto Rico, West Virginia, Missouri, and Massachusetts. The native-born Negroes come from Georgia, Massachusetts, New York, Louisiana, Alabama, Virginia, California, South Carolina, Tennessee, and the Virgin Islands. The foreign-born among us are from Canada, the Philippine Islands, Greece, Honduras, Scotland, the British West Indies, Peru, England, Belgium, and China. We are black, white, yellow, red and brown . . . men from North, Central, and South America . . . men from Asia and Oceania . . . men from Europe . . . men whose forefathers came from Africa. In all my life, which has taken me into a great variety of human situations, I have never been a member of so harmonious a team.

*   *   *

Captain Mulzac is teaching his navigation class on the shelter deck, which "Chips" Reed fixed up like a schoolroom with a blackboard, benches, and desks that fold down from the bulkheads. The skipper has put a long problem on the board, all about azimuths, and the heads puzzle—the blond one of Jim Youngdale, the navy gunnery officer; the kinky one of Ted, the ordinary seaman—all the heads puzzle. Every evening after supper we have classes —Engineering, Mathematics, Cooking and Baking, Radio, Hygiene and First Aid, Seamanship—a ship's meeting or forum on world problems and trade-unionism. The Captain sometimes teaches the class in Cooking and Baking as well as the one on Navigation. On Christmas he rolled up his sleeves and made the plum pudding himself and mixed the hard sauce. It was the best plum pudding you ever tasted. And he baked a huge cake for a Christmas party in his quarters. He had wine and vermouth to go with it. It made us forget how far we were from home and how soon we would be leaving that port for further up the line, with troops and invasion cargo.

CHAPTER SEVEN

Trial

ALL THE WAY down the Mexican and Central American coast on the SS Booker T. Washington's maiden voyage, Navy patrol planes checked on her, to make certain that Captain Mulzac knew his business and was keeping her on the course. After she passed through the Panama Canal into the Caribbean, the skeptical Navy was satisfied and left her alone. The Captain knew these waters like the back of his hand.

When the ship reached New York, the CIO Industrial Union Council gave a banquet for her Captain and crew at the Hotel Commodore. The great ballroom was packed to the walls with guests, white and black, in what was probably the most moving demonstration of inter-racial unity that has yet taken place in America. Here one heard no cautious words about "the need for more education, understanding, and tolerance," no mealy-mouthed protestations that Negroes sought only to develop their "racial potentialities" within the traditional patterns of segregation. Instead, one heard from

Captain Mulzac, Chief Engineer Smith, Ship's Delegate Harry Alexander, and representatives of the all-white Navy gun crew the story of a triumphant working unity already achieved by both races, the confession of a sure faith that the brotherhood of the SS Booker T. Washington would some day embrace all Americans, all peoples.

Then Paul Robeson sang, not Negro songs, but songs of the ordinary people around the world, and his singing made the brotherhood of man come closer and more real than any sermon ever heard upon these shores. Afterwards he spoke, talking about his son. Soon, he said, his son was entering Cornell to study engineering. For Captain Mulzac had inspired the boy with the knowledge that now at last it was possible for a Negro in America to be accepted as a master technician. How many dark-skinned boys, like Paul Robeson's son, look today at Captain Mulzac's picture, clipped from *People's Voice,* the Chicago *Defender,* the Pittsburgh *Courier,* the Baltimore *Afro-American* or the Norfolk *Journal and Guide,* and pasted up on a shabby tenement or cabin wall, taking from it the courage to believe in America, to believe in themselves? The steady eyes, still touched by the sadness of long frustration; the gentle but lasting-looking face; the clean, austere expression; the proud American eagle above the seal and anchor on the cap device; the four broad stripes of gold upon the shoulder boards. "I did it," Captain Mulzac says from his picture on hundreds of thousands of walls where Negro American children are growing up, "and so can you, whatever it is you want to do. But you must study. You must work. You must be loyal. And you must be always ready to stake your life in the service of all your American brothers, white and black, and of all your other brothers around the world, whatever their color, who are not free, as you are."

After the warmth and glow of the banquet, the sea was cold and dark. Bleak Halifax was gripped in ice and full of survivors from lost ships waiting for passage back to the States. They told grim stories of wolf-pack assaults on their convoys and of shipmates whose frozen bodies were left bobbing on the stormy ocean. The men of the SS Booker T. Washington became taut and quiet, waiting for convoy to Britain.

The day came for departure and again they put to sea. Off the Grand Banks of Newfoundland, a terrible gale broke over the convoy. The wind screamed down out of Labrador and the bitter wastes beyond, piling great waves that smashed the wallowing ships full on the beam. A Liberty has no rolling chocks to speak of, and rolls her rails under in a heavy sea. The SS Booker T. Washington was loaded to the plimsoll line and her decks were heaped with cargo—planes, tanks, and massive crates. Green water swept her decks time and again. At nightfall the storm grew worse, and a great wave smashed up to the boat deck, carrying away both starboard lifeboats and breaking down the forward passageway storm door. Tons of water poured into the ship, washing the Chief Engineer out of his bunk, sluicing through the alleyways and cascading down to the lower decks. Instantly the Captain pulled her out of convoy, and ran with the gale until the smashed door could be heavily boarded up. Another such wave might send water crashing down to the engine room, knocking out the engines.

By morning the ship was back in her convoy position. All that day the storm continued, and again grew more fierce at nightfall. The rollers swept over the rails, heaving with powerful shoulders against the planes, tanks, and crates on the decks; wrenching at thick wire-cable lashings and turnbuckles with their million-fingered clutch. A monstrous crate of machinery covering all of No. 3 hatch broke loose from its lashings and slid toward the rail. This now was really danger, for once cargo begins to shift, a ship can founder, going down suddenly as a stone.

Again, Captain Mulzac left convoy and ran southward with the wind. Two days later he ran out of it into fine weather and hauled around. There was no hope of finding the convoy now, so the Captain charted his course for the north of Ireland and told the Chief to give her full throttle. Keeping a 24-hour watch in the crow's nest, as well as lookouts forward, aft and on the flying bridge, with the whole gun crew at standby, the ship raced for seven days. The subs never got on her trail and she rounded Ireland and entered safe waters. As she reached her destination, the harbor patrol boat stopped her with a shot across her bows. When her story was known, the pilot came aboard to take her to the dock. The convoy steamed in two-and-a-half days later, with several ships missing. A wolf pack had jumped them.

The Lord Mayor of the great port city came aboard to honor the ship, while members of the crew were invited into war industrial centers to tell gatherings of British workers about the SS Booker T. Washington. Though she has never returned to Britain, the ship is remembered there as a symbol of American democracy very different from the Jim Crow pattern with which our Army has outraged the common Englishman's sense of justice.

Still later, in the Mediterranean, Captain Mulzac and his officers were entertained by the commander of the Nelson aboard his famous British battleship. No comparable honor has ever been done him by our own Navy. Yet there were men in the American government who could value the heroism and competence displayed by Captain Mulzac on his ship's first voyage into the war zone. The Office of War Information was quick to dramatize the story of how the SS Booker T. Washington met her trial. It was presented on a nationwide broadcast in the series, "The Man Behind the Gun." Millions heard it and, hearing, they were proud of this American ship and her American Captain.

CHAPTER EIGHT

The First

WHEN ALARMS come every night, or several times a night, and you go to sleep with all your clothes on, including your shoes, Leroy King does not. He strips down to the buff and puts on striped pajamas. Walking in on him in his cabin, you see him there propped up in the bunk on both pillows, under the glow of the bedlight, with his face shining clean from the shower and those striped pajamas. He's reading the Bible, one of the Gideon Bibles they put aboard ship and nobody ever reads, but Leroy King does.

Not that he believes all of it. He is not what you would call devout. Reading the Bible is an old habit with him, going back to when he was a boy on a New England farm in the Connecticut Valley. He reads it for literature, and for old time's sake. It also helps him to go to sleep when he comes off watch.

Leroy King is descended from people who founded Northampton, Massachusetts. So is his wife, back home. They both had ancestors who fought in the Revolution. They have one of the oldest homes in town, which has been in the King family since 1744, though it is older than that. His wife could join the D.A.R., only she doesn't believe in it. The D.A.R., the Kings think, has got away from the idea of the American Revolution. It stands for just about the opposite, according to them, of what the Revolution did.

Leroy King was left an orphan boy when he was real small. He was brought up on his grandfather's farm in the valley. He was the youngest of three brothers. The older two worked hard on the farm and went off to theological school, both becoming Episcopalian ministers. But Leroy was a poor student. Of course he didn't have much time to study, working his way through high school as the janitor and doing his farm chores too, and having to walk several miles each way. He failed mathematics and felt there wasn't any use his staying in school after that.

So one day he tied up a small bundle, and nobody noticed when he started for school with it. Only he went to the railroad yards instead of the school and hopped a freight for Boston. There, he shipped out on a tramp steamer as a coal-passer. The tramp went to Frisco, where Leroy jumped, thinking it would be easy to make a living out there. He found out he was wrong. The marine firemen had a union on the coast. But it cost a $50 initiation fee to join, which left him out. His only chance was on foreign ships, which weren't organized. He got a job on one and shuttled between Oregon and Southern California for a few trips. Then he became one of the bindle-stiffs who used to harvest the crops out there, with a small bundle on a stick over their shoulders. He drifted from ranch to ranch. One summer he worked on one in the Sacramento Valley, owned by the Governor. He slept in a shed. They would put out the food for the help on the back porch and you would have to scramble for your share. Hindus, Japs, and Chinese were his fellow-workers. They would take anything and be satisfied.

Leroy got close to the Wobblies, the IWW which he had heard about on shipboard. They wanted a revolution, like in the beginning of America. From what little he had seen, Leroy thought they were right. A revolution was what we needed. Start everything off from scratch again. All the time he was riding the freights, up into Oregon, out to Idaho. You would go to a labor agent in L.A., Frisco, Sacramento, or Portland. You would pay him a dollar and he would give you a letter and a coach ticket to some place where there was work. You would have to have a bedding roll as well as a dollar. The second-hand dealers would sell you one for 50 cents—half a comforter, a pair of used overalls and some worn-out work shoes. The labor agent would look at your hands, to see if they were calloused. If you had a dollar, a bedding roll, and calloused hands, the labor agent would give you a coach ticket to Winnemucca, Nevada. The trick was to ride to some place close to the job, then drop off the train and look for something else. For you couldn't count on the job the labor agent sent you to. The labor agent and the construction foreman were usually in cahoots, so you would be fired in a day or two, and the agent would collect another dollar from the guy who took your place. There were always guys.

Wages back then were $2.25 a day. They took out $1.25 a day, seven days a week, for your bunk and keep. The rest went for tobacco and overalls and work shoes at the store, together with stuff you never bought but had to pay for all the same. In four years, Leroy never managed to save up the $50 he needed to join the marine firemen's union. Finally, he bummed his way back across the continent to Massachusetts. Even the gold watch his grand-father had given him was gone. He had tried to pawn it once in L.A. for $10. It was a nice watch. But the pawnbroker had looked at him contemp-tuously and said, "What makes you so independent? You're broke, ain't you? I'll give you five dollars." He had taken the five.

When he got home, he went to work as a fireman on the Boston and Albany. He lived on his grand-father's farm and shoveled into fire-boxes for nothing until he had four written endorsements from locomotive engineers that he was a good fireman. Then the railroad put him on the payroll. The firemen had a union and he made $25 a week. But it wasn't long until the big mallet compounds came in. They would pull seventy-five cars where the old 4-8-0's would only pull thirty. He got "rolled," along with a lot of other firemen.

His next job was as a stationary-engine fireman in the Holyoke insane asylum. The pay was $14 a week, because the stationary firemen weren't organized like the railroad men. Leroy got busy organizing the guys around the paper and textile mills. Then he put in for an AFL charter. Twelve hours a day the guys were working, seven days a week, for fourteen dollars. He got them organized, though a textile-mill owner had him arrested and brought to his office. Leroy persuaded him that he would be better off if the men were organized. When the first war came, he had been promoted to engineer in the insane asylum.

He left his good job and sailed for France in April, 1917, the first month of the war. In between trips, he went through a new government training course at MIT and won his license as Second Assistant Engineer. Then he made five trips to France for the Army Transport Service, carrying ammunition, aviation gas, trucks, and rations. Once they got into the mine fields off the French coast with three million gallons of high test aboard. The Captain signaled the French Navy, "Come and get me out of here," but they wouldn't. The Captain had to get out the best way he knew how.

After the war, Leroy kept on shipping, as First Assistant Engineer, for he had studied and upgraded his license. But the shipowners began cutting down on seamen's conditions, abrogating the wartime agreements and drawing up new wage-scales on their own terms. Though he was an officer, Leroy King stood with the rest of the seamen and went out on strike with them in 1921. The shipowners laid up three thousand ships and went right on with scab crews. It was just what they wanted.

Leroy King went home to Massachusetts and found a job as engineer for an optical company. They paid him seventy cents an hour, twelve hours a night, seven days a week. He tried to organize the men there, but had no luck. On this job, he took care of six boilers, three turbines, and all the auxiliary apparatus with just one fireman to help him. He had to do all the oiling himself, as well as be the engineer.

He quit and went on to a Holyoke textile mill, where at once he started organizing the guys. The Old Man learned about what this engineer was doing and had him on the carpet.

"You're a disturbing element," the Old Man said.

"If ever I saw a plant that needed a disturbing element," Leroy said, "This is it." He pointed out all the waste and inefficiency in the plant. He said the men were working such long hours and earning so little, they didn't give a damn. He said he knew how to change all that, if the Old Man would recognize the union, meet the demands for an eight-hour day and decent wages.

He wound up as Chief Engineer of that mill. As Chief, he wouldn't OK orders for material from non-union companies, and he had many a run-in with the Old Man about it. The Old Man had come to approve of the union in his mill, for it had got the results Leroy King promised, but he said most of the other AFL unions were just rackets. Leroy gradually came to agree with him and tried to throw the Holyoke paper mills into the CIO, though he had become a Vice President of the State AFL and had held every office in his own local—President, Financial Secretary, and Business Agent.

When this war started, Leroy King was over fifty and had a good job as Chief Engineer of a big paper mill. But he read in the Boston paper that Merchant Marine officers were desperately needed to man the wartime fleet, so he packed his bag and reported. By some fluke, he was assigned as First Assistant Engineer on the SS Booker T. Washington. He had experience enough, and far more than enough knowledge, to be a Chief. But he likes it fine, working under a Negro Chief on the Booker T., and living with men of all races and backgrounds who are united on doing a common job. He stays with us for eighteen months. "The First" we call him simply, and the respect in that is something few Chiefs ever hear in all their experience. He finally gets off to be a Chief on another ship, as he could have done in the beginning.

John King was the first of the American family from which Leroy King is descended. He helped found Northampton in 1654, after coming out with a shipload from England. John King was a farmer and Captain of the Northampton Company which defended the new town against the Indians. Back in England, he had had military experience, fighting for Cromwell's Commonwealth. Another one of his descendants, besides Leroy, was Rufus, who signed the Declaration of Independence in 1776.

CHAPTER NINE

Cadet

OUR CADET, little Joe Williams, is the only man aboard ship who can stand up to Bruce and sometimes get a good lick in. Bruce outweighs him thirty or forty pounds, and Bruce has had years of ring experience, but Joe is out after him every evening in the nice weather, when the boys spar on No. 4 hatch. Everything Bruce knows about fighting, Joe is learning, but that isn't all.

Cadets eat with the officers in the saloon, bunk in officer's quarters, wear gold on their uniforms when they go ashore, and sometimes give themselves airs. But no airs for Joe. On deck, he's just one of the Bos'n's gang in paint-smeared dungarees. When there are booms to be secured, Joe's up there on the mast-head. He stands look-outs on the bow, relieves the wheel, chips paint, washes down the deck like any ordinary seaman. Off watch, he's hard at his books, studying navigation, mathematics, engineering, ship's business—all the things he will need to know when he goes back to the Merchant Marine Academy to finish his training. His last trip with us, Joe moves up to Acting Third Mate when the old gas-hound we got for Third Mate on a pier-head jump has to be left in jail in a foreign port. Joe makes us as good a Third Mate as we have ever had.

Joe comes from Annapolis. The first thing he can remember is watching the dress parades at the Naval Academy. That was where he would be himself some day, he decided, marching in his blues on that fine parade ground. He was too little to know yet that the blackness of his skin made this a hopeless ambition, and that Annapolis cadets weren't chosen from families like his own. His father and mother had separated when he was five. The mother supported Joe and his three sisters on her earnings of $40 a month as cook in a white home. When he was ten, Joe started picking up little jobs. He got a shoeshine box and stood on corners. He would hustle the midshipmen's bags when they went on furlough. He caddied at the Academy golf course for lordly white officers who didn't dream that the tattered little Negro who lugged their heavy clubs and ferreted out their slices from the rough aspired to become one of them some day. They paid him 28 cents for nine holes and 55 cents for eighteen. By the time he was thirteen, Joe was setting up pins in the bowling alley at the Officers' Club, and was beginning to catch on to Jim Crow.

He was a freshman in the colored high school and one of his classes was civics. He studied the Declaration of Independence, the Constitution of the United States and for the first time understood what his rights, as an American, were supposed to be. Then he looked at Jim Crow Annapolis. He thought about the segregated ghetto where he lived and where the only playmates he ever had were Negroes like himself, except for a couple of Jewish boys who used to sneak over into the Negro quarter to play football with them. Joe looked at the Naval Academy with new eyes. It was meant for him, he knew that. The United States Government established it for everybody who could meet its strict standards of scholarship, physique, and character. But he had about as much chance of getting into it

as into the British House of Lords. Joe developed a
burning interest in American history. He wanted
to know why the country was turning out so different from what it was intended to be, what was in
white people's minds that poisoned them against
his people. The history books didn't give him the
answer, though some historical novels gave him
clues. Then he rebelled. It didn't make any difference what the Constitution and the other fine docu-
ments said. The cards were stacked against the
Negro.

Joe quit studying as a sophomore and played
hookey for forty-five straight days. You learned
more about real life, and how you had to get along,
hanging around the poolroom with the gang. They
undertook to teach him how to throw crooked dice,
how to deal off the bottom, how to stack or mark a
deck himself. But he did keep up the sports he had
always loved. There were no athletic fields for
Negroes in Annapolis. They played football in the
back lots, roller-skate hockey with tin cans in the
streets. Joe liked swimming, but all the bathing
beaches were closed to Negroes. He and his crowd
would dive off the railroad trestle and swim there.
When he was a junior, the gang let him in on the
real serious business, "clipping." This was breaking
into stores, which they thought a better way than
caddying or shining shoes, or hustling midshipmen's
bags, to get their lunch money, clothes and change
to spend on girls. On his first job, Joe was posted as

a look-out, but he got scared and ducked out. There was nothing in this, either, he decided, and broke with the gang.

His senior year, Joe went back to his books and finished near the top of his class. Though he was the class Vice President, the star end on the football team and the leading man in the school plays, he still had to hike all over town after school with his shoeshine box to rustle up the 15 cents for his lunch next day and something extra to add to his capital. He was trying to save up $5, which was required as a deposit with his application to Hampton Institute in Virginia. By May, he had the $5 and sent it to Hampton.

When he graduated from high school in June, Joe had exactly $1, the gift of a cousin. But he was determined to get to Hampton in the fall. Every day for a month, he hunted a job, and finally he landed one as a waiter in a café, only to lose it immediately when a swinging door knocked a tray of dishes out of his hands. He was demoted to bus-boy but finished the summer with $65 saved. His mother borrowed $75 on her burial policy, the family's only resource, and Joe set out for Hampton. He had enough for his uniform, shoes, books, and tuition. He figured he could get along somehow, and did.

At Hampton, Joe washed dishes, swept the gymnasium, cleaned up the athletic field, anything he could get to do that would keep him there. He made the football team in his sophomore year and was a regular for three years. In the summers he worked, one summer aboard ship on the Philadelphia-Boston run, as a messboy. He helped to organize the NMU aboard, sneaking union literature on the ship in laundry sacks. The skipper tried to break it up, but the union won the election in September. The next summer Joe worked at the Rogers Rock Club on Lake George, as a bellhop, and for the first time in his life he met "white people who treated you like a human being."

At Hampton, Joe's ambition to get into the Naval Academy reawakened. He knew what it would mean, if he managed to force himself in—unadulterated hell his plebe year and, after that, three years of boycott. When he received his bachelor's degree from Hampton, Congressman Mitchell of Illinois, a Negro, appointed him to the Academy. Though Joe was far better prepared than most appointees, he was rejected on the specious grounds that his required mathematics had been taken three years or more previously and hence could not be counted. He was not given the opportunity of standing a competitive examination. Joe put his degree and his hopes of becoming a Navy officer away in the old trunk and went to work with a wheelbarrow, on a housing project. Then a teaching job turned up, in a colored high school in rural Maryland. While there, he heard about the United States Merchant Marine Academy and made application. He was accepted.

The Navy officer in charge of the enrolling office in New York tried to discourage him, frankly telling him that he would be the only Negro in the Academy and that the other cadets would make life miserable for him. But Joe looked at him steadily and said he could take whatever was in store for him. On the train up to the Academy, he got close to five white fellows who were also entering. They accepted him as one of themselves. Two of them came from Massachusetts, but the other three were from Texas, Virginia, and Missouri. They agreed to stick together and, when they arrived, were all put into a new section of twenty-five.

The staring, whispering, and threatening started immediately. One of the Massachusetts boys, who had been made section leader, was called out by the upperclassmen the first night and taken to their dorm. They told him it was up to the section to run the "nigger" out. The next night all five of Joe's white friends were given a going-over. They wouldn't scare, so the upperclassmen came after Joe himself. Pack up, they told him, before he got the works. Joe said he wouldn't pack up and what were they going to do about it? They said he'd soon see.

Again the section leader was called out. Every man in the section would be treated as a "nigger" unless Joe was chased out. OK, the section leader said, and when he told the other guys the story, they backed him—twenty-four white boys from all over the union, many from the South. OK, they said, we'll be "niggers."

Backhandedly, the Navy officers in charge of the Academy endorsed the boycott against Joe. Every cadet, upon admission, was automatically sworn into the Naval Reserve. When graduated, the cadets received commissions as officers in the Naval Reserve. But the Navy pointedly left Joe out, as he alone in the whole Academy was not entitled to wear the proud gold wings of the USNR on his blouse.

First, the members of the section were subjected to a freeze campaign: none of the other cadets would talk or associate with them. When their front didn't break, the upperclassmen got together. The section's quarters in the dorm were raided by parties of "inspectors," who found cause to shower down demerits. Cadet officers gave section members demerits for the slightest mistakes at drill. Then a Jewish boy came to Joe and told him that the whole business didn't represent how the fellows really felt, but was the work of a ringleader, a highranking cadet officer from the Panama Canal Zone. Joe went straight to him and talked things over. The cadet officer said he wasn't going to permit any Negro to stay in the Academy, and that was that. Joe said he wasn't going to let any white man run him out. They shook hands on their mutual resolve to "get" each other, the cadet officer saying Joe's was the first black hand he had ever shaken.

It ended up with Joe "getting" the cadet officer. The boycott fell of its own weight, and the fellows came over to Joe, ashamed of what they had done. All the while, the Navy officers in charge had not lifted a finger to discipline the cadets organizing the trouble. They may have figured that Joe couldn't stand the pressure and would withdraw, saving them the headache of placing him as an officer on a ship. But Joe knew he wasn't sticking there just for his own sake. If he had quit, his case would have become the authorities' airtight excuse for excluding all Negroes in the future. When Joe left to join the SS Booker T. Washington, he was one of the most popular and respected cadets in the Academy.

In his first foreign port, Joe bumps into the Massachusetts boy who stood up for him when he entered the Academy. Together with a paratrooper lieutenant we have brought over, they make all the bars like any three boys ashore for the first time on foreign soil. Joe also finds on the docks four Negro friends who went to Hampton with him. They are all enlisted men in an Army port battalion, unloading cargo as ordinary stevedores, though two of them were math majors and had applied for the artillery.

After ten months on the Booker T. Washington, Joe goes back to the Academy and finishes his course, getting his mate's license with honors. But he doesn't return to the Merchant Marine. At last throwing over its tradition against commissioning

Negroes, the Navy is accepting them as officers. And Joe is one of the first Negro Ensigns. He's gone out to the South Pacific, in the Seabees.

I have an idea Joe's success story is just beginning. If he gets that girl he introduced me to, who works at the USO in Annapolis, so poised and so unconscious of her great beauty, they will go places together.

CHAPTER TEN

Mac and I

FROM WHERE OUR SHIP is anchored at the buoys in the outer port, we can see the people winding along the steep paths down the cliffs to the Mediterranean. Once down, they sun themselves on the rocks and splash in the sea. After you have been aboard ship for many lonely weeks, to see people makes you incredibly happy and restless. Whoever they may be, you want to get to know them, to be with them. Clinging to the cliff are flimsy shacks and cottages, summer places, and at the base a pavilion marked "Brasserie." The word means bar, I tell the guys, but "Sparks" Blackman won't take it that way, insisting that it really is "Brassiere" and letting his imagination run riot on what is going on inside.

Mac, the Negro Third Mate, and I go ashore to explore the cliffs the next day. We want to know what's in these people's minds, how they live, what they want. The bum-boat threads through the ships and bombed wrecks in the inner harbor to the landing. From the city, we take a tram-car back to the faubourg above the cliffs. It is Sunday and the paths swarm with the polyglot population of the town—French, Arab, Spanish, Jewish. We can hear phonographs playing cracked and happy tunes inside the flimsy shacks, and the laughter of women. Through windows, we see couples dancing. In the shade of the cliff, a family is having a picnic. At the bottom a patriarchal Arab sits on the crest of a boulder while his shrouded womenfolk dabble their bare feet in the water. Naked kids frisk in the sea. We are in the midst of people, yet not of them. "Pardon, messieurs," is all they say as they brush past us on the path.

"Brassiere" turns out to be just a dingy little beer joint, but there are tables looking over the sea and the ships at anchor. We sit down and the waiter comes over apologetically. He regrets that he cannot serve us. We ask about the people drinking beer at the other tables and he points to a sign over the bar, "U.S. FORCES MAY BE SERVED ONLY BETWEEN 1100 - 1300 AND 17 - 1900 HOURS." There is nothing that would give him greater pleasure than serving us, the waiter says, but the military authorities are very strict and will close his place if he violates the rules. We may stay at our table and regard the beauty of the sea if we desire until five o'clock, when it will be permitted to serve us beer. We thank him and go, slowly climbing the golden cliffs past the shacks where phonographs are playing and women are laughing.

"I wonder what our wives are doing today," Mac says. "It's Sunday."

"The same thing we are, I guess. Walking around, trying to forget how lonely they are."

"Some guys worry about their wives," Mac says, "about their going out with Jody." (Jody is the mythical character who takes care of seamen's wives and girl friends while they are away. He is pictured wearing the bathrobe, pajamas and bedroom slippers you carefully put away when you left.)

"I guess some have good reason to worry," I say. "Or else they have guilty consciences."

"Jody doesn't bother me," Mac says, "not with the kind of wife I have. But I surely miss her."

"It's tough," I say.

"It's the only thing I mind about this," Mac says. "Boy, if she were only here, what a time we'd

have exploring everything. The least thing is fun
when she's with me. We don't even have to take a
drink."

"Yes," I say, "the least thing is fun." We go on
clambering up the cliff and I try to picture my
Virginia and the children out in Van Courtlandt
Park today, or over on the Palisades, but their
faces seem dim and sad.

Mac and I wander up and down the streets of
the faubourg and wind up in a small bar. We are
very thirsty. By now, luckily, it is between "1700
and 1900 hours." The place is crowded with GI's,
all white, who are quartered nearby. Mac and I
are wearing our brassbound uniforms, and they
look us over with disbelief, never having seen the
like, a white and a Negro officer drinking together
and talking with complete unrestraint like any two
friends.

Mac pushes money across the counter to pay for
our beers, but a GI pushes it back to him. "This is
on me," he says. Mac and I don't get out of there
until we've been treated to far more beers than we
need, from GI's who won't take no for an answer.
One follows us out, a tough Southerner, brother of
a famous University of Alabama football player.
He grabs Mac's arm and takes us down the street
to meet a wonderful Spanish family he knows.
They are Loyalist refugees, with a daughter whom
the Southerner considers the most beautiful person
on earth and the only woman for him.

The Spanish people send out for salt fish, bread, tomatoes, and wine—fiercely rejecting our money —and we have dinner with them. Mac with his sailor's Spanish and I with my almost forgotten French tell the girl and her family what a great guy the tough Southerner is. They agree, for he got medicine from the army hospital for grandmother when she was so sick, and he brings chocolate bars for the children and cans of C rations. But the girl positively will not go to the movies with him. She has a husband in one of Franco's concentration camps. She had a husband, that is, six years ago when he went in, but he might still be living, and she is waiting to see.

The old man had a good job in Spain before Franco chased him out because he was for the Republic. Since coming here, he has been working as a clerk for a Frenchman with a foundry in town. This French employer is a fascist and was all for Vichy before the Ameicans came in. He denounced a lot of his workers and had them shot or put in concentration camps. Then he cut the wages of the rest and nobody dared to protest. The Frenchman's still for Vichy, though he keeps his mouth shut, and gets lots of work from the Americans, at big prices. But he still pays the old Spaniard the same wages—$8 a week. We translate the story for the tough Southerner and he bristles up. "Where is the foundry?" he roars. "I'll get some of my guys and we'll take the place apart. Make the old man tell you where it is. I'll break the Frenchman's God damn fascist neck."

He really means it and Mac has to reason with him a long time, filling his glass up again and again, and pointing out how it would only do the old man harm, as well as himself, if he took the joint apart and broke the Frenchman's God damn fascist neck. "You got to take it easy," Mac says.

"The hell with that," the Southerner says. "I came over here to kill these fascist bastards, wherever I find 'em. And we're giving business to the no-good son of a bitch. His gang shot at us, when we landed here, after they'd promised not to, the double-crossing bastards, and they killed a lot of my buddies."

"That's right," Mac says, "but that doesn't make it right for you to do something that will get you court-martialed and maybe shot yourself. Cool off. We'll take care of these fascists some day, or their own people will take care of them after we leave."

"What's going to happen to fascists like your employer after the Americans leave?" I ask the old man in French.

He smiles in a grim way and slowly draws the side of his hand across his throat.

I am watching the girl. She seemed almost colorless when I came in but she grows on me. She is delicately formed, gray-eyed, subdued. I try once again to plead the Southerner's cause, for I promised him.

"He's a fine man," I say in French, pointing.

"Yes," she agrees with warm eyes, "so strong and honest."

"He says . . ." and I hesitate, "He says you are the finest woman he has ever known."

"I am very happy," she says but I can see very clearly that she is not. "If he thinks I am so fine a woman, it is because . . . because I have so fine a husband. He also is strong and honest. That is why he fought the fascists. That is why they put him in jail. They had fear of him."

"How long has it been since you had news of him?"

"Six years," she says. "We have heard nothing since his imprisonment."

And then I see the woman the Southerner had seen, beautiful as the Madonnas of the old painters and just as holy, though alive.

"It's no good," I tell the Southerner when we leave. "She loves her husband."

"But he's dead!" the Southerner says.

"No doubt," I say. "He was strong and honest and the fascists feared him. When they catch people like that, they always kill them. She knows that. But still she loves him. His being dead doesn't make any difference."

"Dead six years," the Southerner says, "and she won't even forget him long enough to go to the movies with me. All I want is to take her to the movies, be with her, see her laugh a little, get her mind off her troubles. Hell, I wouldn't touch her any more than I would my own sister. I mean of course I love her, I mean . . . God damn it, I want to marry the girl."

"Well," I said. "You see how it is."

"I guess I'll just have to get drunk and get me some hump," he says. "I got some good hump lined up. You guys like some good humping?"

"No, thanks," I say.

"No, thanks," Mac says.

"Well, so long, you guys," he says. So long, we tell him, but he lingers. "Mac," he says, "where I come from we wouldn't give a guy like you a chance. This is the first time in my life I ever drank or sat down at the same table with a Negro. But I want you to know this. If you ever get down my way after this is over, I want you to come and see me and things will be just like they were to-night. And if anybody down there doesn't like it, they'll have me to whip. I never met a finer guy than you are, Mac. Jesus, I wish the Army was like your ship must be."

CHAPTER ELEVEN

Cracker

H E WANTS to make trouble from the beginning, but when he discovers that everybody is against him, he proceeds with caution. He's what the Negroes in the deep South call a cracker, meaning by that a worthless white man who nevertheless holds himself superior to any Negro. This cracker is a fireman we signed on in Norfolk who comes from farther down yet. Other white Southerners in this and earlier crews harmonize with our ship as well as, or better than, most white Northerners. Take "Pop" Miller in the Navy gun crew, a former plantation overseer from the Georgia low country, who is everybody's pal and starred at the dance we gave our Navy crew in the Baltimore NMU ball. Or take Hooker, the tough little AB from the Blue Ridge mountains. "Hook" tags around after Bruce Shepard, our Negro bos'n, a topflight heavyweight who fought Bob Pastor in the Garden. Bruce spars with him every evening on the hatch, giving the little guy pointers, which "Hook" puts to good use when he goes ashore with Bruce in foreign ports. Just let somebody make something out of it when he and Bruce go in a bar together. No matter how big they are, they're "Hook's" meat. He laid out ten in one port.

What burns the cracker is working under a Negro chief engineer, but he starts his trouble in a roundabout way. He sets about building himself up as a champion of the merchant crew against the "gold braid" and the Navy boys. He is always on the look-out for "beefs," which he tries to blow up to monstrous proportions. First it is the mess-room "beef." The merchant crew ought to have the bigger of the two mess-rooms, he says. It's theirs by rights and not the Navy's. So it is, but the first crew ever to sail on the ship voted to let the Navy have the big room, as a gesture of good will. However it may be on other ships, on the SS Booker T. Washington the Navy gun crew are members of the family. They come to our classes and forums, have a part in putting on our shows, contribute to our ship's paper. When the general alarm rings, we man the guns beside them. When we go ashore in port, looking for a little fun, we all go together. So the cracker doesn't get to first base with this beef. The guys shout him down in meeting. "Hell, no," they tell him. "Sure, it's our mess-room, but we gave it to them, see?"

Next, the cracker comes to me about the slop chest. This is a big locker where twice a week I sell cigarettes, tobacco, dungarees, socks, shoes and such to all the guys. He doesn't think it's right, he says, for me to sell stuff to the Navy boys. I ask him why not. Well, he says, they've got their own small stores ashore. They ought to take care of what they need before they come aboard and not buy stuff intended for the merchant crew. I tell him the stuff in the slop was put on for everybody, and first come, first served.

His last ship was different, the cracker says. The Navy only got what was left over after the merchant crew had their pick of the stuff. So I have to remind him that this isn't his last ship, and he'd better find out how we do things, and learn to like it. I tell him the Navy boys like it well enough to forego twenty-one day leaves in order to stay aboard us. For three trips, we didn't lose a Navy boy from the gun crew, and we'd still have most of them if the Navy brasshats hadn't decided there was something suspicious about their liking the ship so well, replacing every last one of them before this trip.

The cracker thinks up a few more phony beefs which he airs in meeting only to get stepped on by the guys. All but Larry, the Boston Irishman. Somehow, the cracker has got hold of him. Larry has been on quite a number of trips. His pal is Antonio, the Spanish oiler. They always stick together aboard ship and ashore. Larry has a boy's face over a body like a bear's. He hasn't been going to sea long, but he has been coming along so well that he was elected engine-room delegate this trip. But something's happening. The cracker pipes down in meetings, or doesn't even come. And Larry does the phony beefing. The guys notice that Larry is staying away from Antonio and is always hanging around the cracker's fo'c'sle when he's off watch. They shut the door while they're inside, something guys seldom do aboard ship.

When we get to Italy, Larry leaves Antonio in the lurch and goes ashore with the cracker. Then Larry comes back alone. The cracker's in the Army hospital, he says. They were just going quietly along one of those narrow alleys after dark and a bunch of Italians jumped them. Larry hasn't a mark on him but he says the cracker's in bad shape.

When the cracker comes back aboard two days later, his nose is completely galley-west, the whole bridge smashed flat. Strangely, he's off Larry and won't speak to him. Larry breaks down and tells the story. He says he fell for the cracker's phony line for a while. Then he got more and more fed up. The guy kept needling him, about being bossed by "niggers" and crap like that. The cracker said everybody aboard was just a bunch of communists and a good Irish Catholic like Larry had no business hanging around with a dirty Spanish Red like Antonio who had probably raped a bunch of nuns during the Civil War. All of a sudden Larry got enough of it. They were just walking down an alley with the cracker buzzing his phony line and

Larry hauled off and socked him once, wrecking his nose. When the cracker came to, Harry dragged him to the Army hospital and left him there.

After that, the cracker hasn't anybody he can buzz to. In Sicily he goes ashore by himself and gets drunk alone. He comes around to my room, drunk. He wants to explain himself, because nobody understands him. I am an intelligent man, and I will understand him. Didn't I use to be editor of some paper, very left-wing, he asks me cagily. He names a paper I never heard of. "Hell no," I tell him, "I don't believe there is any such paper." Well, maybe not, he says, but anyway I am very intelligent and I will understand him, being a white man myself. "Yeah?" The thing of it is this, he says confidentially. He's from the South, but that doesn't make him against "niggers." Oh no. He's for 'em. He wants to see 'em get ahead, have a square deal. He clucks his tongue in sympathy for what the Negro race has suffered. But, he says, they ought to stick to their own women and not go bothering white women.

"Who bothers white women?" I ask him.

"They all do. They all want to, if they don't."

"Bunk."

"You oughta see how these white women over here go for them. Why, they'd rather have them than white men."

"You come from down South," I say. "I suppose you've never had a colored woman?"

"Sure," he says, "lots of times. Why I'd rather have one than a white——"

"I guess you go around bothering them," I say.

"No," he says. "They're willing."

"Well, these white women you're talking about over here are willing. That's their business, isn't it?"

"I wouldn't mind it so much if the niggers didn't boast about it," he says. "That's not right. Boasting about some blond."

"Of course you wouldn't boast about some colored woman?"

"Well——"

"And who does all this boasting about some blond anyway?"

"The colored fellows on this ship."

"I never heard them," I say. "I've been on this ship a lot longer than you have and nobody ever boasted in my hearing. Go on, tell me their names."

"Well," he says, "I've heard 'em but I don't remember who."

"You better hit the sack," I say, "and, for your sake, I don't remember what you said to me. But if I were you I'd lay off this phony line before somebody sends you back to the hospital for keeps."

He goes ashore again alone and fails to show up for his night watch. We're pulling away from the dock, too, out into the stream. It's late the next afternoon when the British Navy launch brings him out to the ship. He's so gassed up he can't climb the Jacob's ladder and we have to haul him aboard in a bos'n's chair. On the following day the Captain, Chief Engineer and I try him. He's disrated from fireman to wiper, the lowest job in the engine room. Sam, a hard-working and fast-learning Negro wiper, is promoted to his old place. The cracker has no defense and signs the log-book, after mumbling something about wanting "another chance."

"You're getting it," the Captain says. "I could have put you ashore here and locked up for jumping ship. Most captains would."

When we are within a week from home the cracker takes to his bunk. The heavy work of wiping has given him a heart attack, he says. His heart didn't bother him when he was firing because all he had to do was just stand on the floorplates and watch his boilers. I can't find anything wrong about him but, to be on the safe side, we let him stay in his bunk. We figure the cracker is trying to make some sort of suit out of it. When we get in, the Coast Guard inspectors uphold the disrating and the cracker pays off. Nobody even tells him good-bye.

A year later the Captain bumps into him in Norfolk, where we're about to sail. The cracker comes rushing up to ask him for a job. He says he will take a wiper's job, anything. He tells the Captain that he got everything that was coming to him on that trip with us. He says he has been on a lot of ships since and he has learned what a good ship is. He says if the Captain will only let him back on the SS Booker T. Washington, he'll show he means every word he's saying, and he'll stay on her all the rest of the war.

If he didn't have a full crew already, Captain Mulzac would give the guy a second chance.

CHAPTER TWELVE

Stateless

I HAVE A PICTURE over my desk of my wife and myself looking at each other. It is just an unfinished print, but it was taken by a man who cared about us both, and he got that into it. It is the only one we have, and the man who took it lost his life as a direct consequence of this war, so we prize it. One trip I have it over my desk at sea. The next trip it is Virginia's turn, and she has it over her desk back home.

John Carapiet, the desk engineer, keeps coming in my room on one pretext or another, and sitting where he can look at the picture. One day he says it ought not to be tacked up like that, but should have a frame. He says he will make a frame for it if I will let him. He spends hours carving out a frame back aft on the fan-tail. When he brings it back finished, we get talking and this dark, taciturn man tells me his story.

Carapiet is down on the articles as a Persian, but he has nothing to prove it, no birth certificate, no passport, no anything. He belongs nowhere and never has belonged anywhere in all his thirty-three years. So far as he knows, he hasn't a living relative.

His father was an Armenian carpenter from Tiflis in the Russian Caucasus, Stalin's native country, who got mixed up in the abortive revolution of 1905 and fled to Teheran to escape the Czar's police. John Carapiet was born there but when he was five his father fled again with the British Consul, taking his family to India for safety against the threatened persecution of Armenians in Persia after the outbreak of the First World War. When he was still small his father died and Carapiet went to work on the Indian railroads. He became a shunter, making up trains. But he wasn't satisfied. He switched from the railroads to firing on Ganges River steamers. Then he sailed deep sea for four years, running from India to China, Japan and the East Indies. When he knew all the East, he changed to the British run.

His first torpedoing came right after the outbreak of the war, off the Irish coast. For fifteen days he tossed on the heavy seas, in a lifeboat with eight shipmates, one of whom died from exposure before they were picked up by a Greek freighter bound for Capetown, South Africa. Carapiet got a ship back to India, and chose the Halifax-Calcutta run. His ship took a bomb right down her stack at Birkenhead during the blitz of Britain. Nearly everybody was killed, but John happened to be ashore. When he got back to his ship, only her masts were there, sticking up out of the water alongside the dock.

These were just the risks of the game and Carapiet kept shipping. He was at Singapore on December 7, 1941 when the Japs struck at Pearl Harbor. A few months later his second torpedoing sank his ship from under him right in Halifax harbor. There was no time to launch lifeboats. He was swimming ashore in the icy water when a police launch picked him up. The most perilous run at this time was to Murmansk, and Carapiet decided he would chance it. He liked the fight the Russians were putting up and wanted to help them.

He went over to the United States Lines and started shipping to Murmansk. Four straight times he made it over and back safely through everything the Nazis planes and subs based in Norway and Finland could throw at him. One time, almost the entire convoy was knocked off. On every run, ships were sunk all around him. The fifth time he didn't make it. His ship was torpedoed right off Halifax. It was winter and the seas were heavy, but they managed to launch the boats. Another freighter picked them up and Carapiet had just climbed to her deck and was drinking the shot of rum handed out to warm him up when that ship was hit. Carapiet and the others swarmed down the nets into the boat and again they rode the giant waves. This time a hospital ship rescued him. He was returned to Halifax, where the United States Lines agent gave him transportation to New York to pick up another ship. They valued this man who knew his job and wouldn't scare.

When Carapiet got to New York, the Immigration officials arrested him. It wasn't enough that he had been sent into the country by an agency of our own government, not enough that he had proved his loyalty to the Allied cause by continuing to sail after four torpedoings and a bombing, not enough that he was a highly skilled seaman whose services were desperately needed to keep the cargoes moving to the front. He had no papers proving that he was a citizen of an Allied or a neutral country. The Immigration Service was not at that time concerned with the record of a seaman, only with his papers. If he had no papers, lock him up.

Carapiet was interned on Ellis Island, along with five thousand other seamen, there and at Rikers Island, mainly men who had jumped foreign ships in American ports long years before and had settled down ashore. All nationalities were represented, and all the precious seafaring skills. Among the internees were Captains, Chief Engineers, Mates. They were evidently considered to be dangerous men, for armed guards were posted on the gallery when they ate their meals.

Carapiet was there for six months. During his imprisonment he kept busy, cutting the other internees' hair, running a candy and cigarette stand, mending clothes, doing washings. In the six months, he saved nine hundred dollars. Then his health broke down, and he was put in the hospital for a month and a half.

When he was ready to leave the hospital, the Immigration authorities relented toward him. He could sail, provided he kept sailing. He was escorted aboard a ship and an armed guard posted over him to keep him aboard until sailing time. Carapiet demanded that either he be sent back to jail or the guard be removed, and the Captain backed him up. The guard was removed. The ship was supposedly bound for Murmansk, but she turned around in Bermuda and, disgusted, Carapiet piled off when she got in and shipped to North Africa and England for a couple of trips. Then he joined the SS Booker T. Washington. This is his second voyage with us. In all this time, I am the first to whom he has told his story.

Carapiet has nine thousand dollars saved up in the bank. A girl in Calcutta got him started saving a long time ago. They were engaged. Carapiet said he would come back and marry her when he had enough put aside to start a little business there, importing and exporting in a small way. But he hasn't heard from the girl since he was in Calcutta years ago. She is an Armenian too. Now Carapiet saves just to be saving. There is an Irish policeman's daughter in Baltimore that he likes mighty well. My wife's picture reminds him of her. But she doesn't want to leave America, and the Immigration people won't let Carapiet stay, so he doesn't know what.

When we get near port, Carapiet spends his spare time cutting the crew's hair on the deck. Nobody wants to go ashore all shaggy, and Carapiet is a good barber. He charges full shore prices and makes quite a sum each trip. When he hits the States, he gives it all to the Red Cross. The reason is, he says, that the Red Cross takes care of people who are driven out of their homes and have no country they can call their own.

Our last ship's meeting this trip we pass a resolution asking Congress to confer United States citizenship on men like John Carapiet whose skill, courage and devotion have helped to keep American ships sailing through the most dangerous seas in history. Of course we don't expect to hear from Congress. We don't, that is, unless a whole lot of Americans get the same idea as ours.

CHAPTER THIRTEEN

Brothers

Going across, we take up a collection aboard ship for the Spanish fighters against fascism who are still in French North African jails after six months of American occupation. It is Alex Treskin's idea in the first place. Treskin is our Second Assistant Engineer, but getting to be an officer hasn't made him forget that he came out of the fo'c'sle, or that the ordinary guys of the world are his brothers.

"We have got to prove to these guys in jail," he tells the ship's meeting, "that we Americans haven't forgotten them, even if our authorities have. They were in there fighting our battle against fascism before the rest of us waked up. And they're still in jail for that, while the French fascists who put them there are walking around on the outside."

The collection is a good one—about sixty cartons of cigarettes, a lot of shoes, dungarees, soap, pipes, and tobacco. "Chips" Reed, Harry Alexander, and I are elected as a committee to deliver the stuff when we get into port. It will be up to us to find the right guys and see that they get it, no easy job, we discover.

We talk to one fellow in a French Army hospital. He is there because he has no legs. Three times they had to amputate, finally chopping them off so short they are barely stumps. He is an anti-Nazi Austrian who fought in Spain. He escaped to North Africa and joined the French Foreign Legion after the fall of the republic. He fought for France in 1940, only to be locked up by the Vichyites after the Armistice. They put him to work on the Trans-Saharan Railroad, somewhere south of Colomb-Béchar in the desert, building a line to Dakar for Hitler to use when he got around to invading South America. While there, the soldier fell sick and was transferred to a concentration camp in the Atlas Mountains. It was winter and very cold up there. The commandant of the camp decided that he was malingering and sent him out to break rocks. When he fainted on the job, he was told that obviously he was no good for anything and would be better off dead. They showed him a freshly dug grave. They told him it was his, and to get in it. For six days they kept him lying in it, with an Arab sentry over him. They wouldn't even let him get up to attend to himself. It was cold and there was water in the grave. After the six days they carried him back to the camp and performed the first amputation on his legs, which had been frozen in the grave. Then they transferred him to a French Army hospital, since he had been a French soldier after all. There the other two amputations were performed.

He has a cot to sleep on, a wheelchair to go out on the grounds, and a single shirt. They haven't issued him a uniform. He gets no tobacco allowance. He receives no pay at all, let alone pension. And this six months after the Americans have come in. He finds it difficult to understand why the Vichyite officers still remain in charge of the hospital, why the Americans have not changed all that.

French democrats we talk to on the outside are all asking the same question. They say nobody has been changed from the Vichyite governor down to the Vichyite corner policeman. They all want to know why. The little Frenchman who waits on tables in the American Red Cross club and wears an ARC pin on his lapel tells us the Vichyite police picked him up last night on his way home from work. They took him to the station, into a back room, where they beat him up, telling him that was just a taste of what he was going to get after the Americans were chased out. Anybody who had worked for the Americans was going to have his throat cut, they told him.

The American consul smiles indulgently when we ask him where we can find the Spanish Loyalists who are still in jail. Evidently, he says, we believe all that stuff in the newspapers back home. The story has been grossly exaggerated, he continues, and all the prisoners have been freed.

We later find a young American official who knows the score. He has visited all the camps personally, and arranged for the release of many of the prisoners. But some three hundred to four hundred prisoners have disappeared entirely, and are probably still being worked on the Trans-Saharan railroad deep in the desert south of Colomb-Béchar. And there is a group of about sixty—carefully culled out of the camps because of their qualities of leadership—at present immured in the main penitentiary of Morocco. He has been unable to get permission from the French authorities to visit them. We suggest that they are just the men we are looking for to receive our collection. He smiles and says he doesn't think we will have any luck, but he will do what he can.

The next day we set out with him for Rabat, the capital of Morocco, in an American staff car. Our collection is piled in the trunk and on the back seat floor. The MP's wave us through the control stations outside the towns. The country is full of American encampments, and Rabat swarms with American paratroopers, tied down there by the imminent threat of an invasion across our ocean supply lines through Spanish Morocco. Franco is reported to have heavy forces concentrated along the border. Everybody is expecting Hitler to hurdle the Pyrenees any day now in an attempt to trap the Americans in North Africa, with the aid of his ally, Franco.

We bluff our way past the Vichyite Chief of Security in Rabat, by telling him we represent the American people who have sent these cigarettes and this clothing to their brothers, the Spanish fighters against fascism who are still in his jail. He looks at "Chips" Reed, Deck Engineer Harry Alexander, and myself and we can see him break with fear, believing that we do really represent the American people. We tell him that we don't trust him to deliver the cigarettes and the clothing; that the American people instructed us to hand them over in person to the Spanish prisoners themselves. With his Director of Penal Institutions as escort, we drive on across country to the great penitentiary and find the men we are looking for. We meet them assembled in a big room with barred windows. They wear rough gray homespun from the prison workshop with a big T (for *"Travail Forcé"*) on their breasts. Down the corridor are the prison kitchens, and the stink comes to us of the rotten food cooking. The men are quiet and upright, and their eyes are steady. We tell them our gifts come from their brothers in America in gratitude for their fight against the common enemy. They answer that all they want their brothers in America to do for them is to get them out of there and back into the fight. They have been offered their release if they will accept passage to Mexico, but have refused it. All they want is the chance to fight again, alongside their American brothers.

CHAPTER FOURTEEN

Unity in Tunisia

"THIS SHIP is blessed," Chief Engineer John Garrett keeps saying. "There can't anything happen to her with so many millions of people praying for her every night."

That's his way of explaining all the close squeezes we've got out of. Maybe he's right. Or maybe it's just luck. Myself, I think Captain Mulzac's skill as a navigator has got a lot to do with it. And the black gang's meticulous care of the engines. All those days in port they swung the sledges and wielded the big wrenches, taking things down, adjusting, putting them back together. Those days paid off big at sea in the long transatlantic stretches when for weeks on end the nor'wester pounded our homeward bound convoy, the light ships rolling like so many empty tin cans, their screws jumping clean out of the water as each wave was breasted and whirring up to terrific speed with no water to bite on. No ship is built to run light, without cargo to keep her down in the water, but there isn't anything to bring back from the places we've been going to and so we have to. The engines take an awful beating with the ship behaving like an empty tin can and the screw jumping out every wave. You can tell the engines that haven't been kept up right. The ships they're in suddenly drop back, rolling helplessly in the beam-on seas and are lost over the horizon in the misty gray of the storm while the convoy plows on without them. And the Commodore signals: OUR SPEED 9.5 KNOTS. DISABLED SHIPS TAKE STRAGGLER'S ROUTE. ENEMY SUBMARINES ARE FOLLOWING US.

Not once in more than two years have the engines of the SS Booker T. Washington stopped kicking when they were needed. And not that night when a noise like the end of the world wakes me up. For some reason I had a hunch to sleep in my clothes but I hadn't heeded it. I can hear the men already out on deck, assembling at the boats, while the general alarm keeps clanging. It seems hours while I lace and tie my shoes, but I keep the lid on myself and mentally tick off everything . . . all my papers hitched to my belt by a chain, sheepskin coat because it's cold, gloves for the same reason rummaged out of the bottom of a drawer. Only when I get out on deck do I realize that I have forgotten something—my life preserver.

Water gurgles into a big tear in the starboard side, and oil wells out, coating the waves with shine in the beams of the emergency lights which have been turned on. On the forward deck the troops we're carrying are lined up in their life jackets, waiting to take to the doughnut rafts. In these seas, they won't have much of a chance. Two of our four boats have been carried away in the smash, so nobody's any better off. The engine room must be flooded by this time, and I duck down to reconnoiter. Down and down the spiraling ladder into the oily heat.

Water is just washing over the engine room floorplates. She rolls to starboard, and a wave breaks in. Steam fumes thickly from the hot boiler surfaces where the spray hits. Leroy King, the First Assistant who's on watch, sloshes around in the water, intently picking up buckets full of the black gang's dirty clothes. He carefully places each one out of the sea water's way, on a bench or hanging from a bulkhead. "Hello," he says when he sees me, just as he always does when I come down below, and sloshes toward another bucket.

The underwater damage is right opposite the starboard settler tank. Another two or three feet and we'd have been finished. But the settler tank holds like a second ship's side and all the water we take is through the break over it, above the water line except when we roll to starboard and the sea washes in.

The second day afterwards we make it into a Tunisian port, threading our way, crippled as we are, through a narrow channel clogged with sunken hulks. The port is a bombed-out shell, where not a single civilian lives any more, but only the Army.

Our troops file off and the GI stevedores discharge our cargo: it is destined for a beach-head, but we can't make it now that we're fit only for drydock.

When they've discharged us, we go on to the naval base and arsenal, where there's a big drydock and a town with people in it. Being around there so long, while they work on our ship, we go ashore and find what seamen call "homes." Mine is with a young French family of three—a guy who was in the Navy and now is a machinist in the arsenal, his Parisian wife and their six months old baby. They used to live in the bombed-out port, but their house was destroyed by a direct hit. When the baby was three days old, they started taking it to the slit trench to get away from our bombs. But they welcomed them nevertheless. And then they welcomed our troops, though a lot of things have happened since which they can't understand. This family live in a place called for some reason, *"Cité de la Jeunesse,"* (City of Youth). It was first built as a quarter for bachelor workers in the arsenal. Each apartment consists of a single room. Down the street is the common open-air toilet. Up the street is the water spigot. They sleep, cook, eat, and otherwise live in their one room, and are happy because they still believe in the future despite everything they have seen.

On Sunday they have me to dinner, with a black-market roast cooked on their single gas-burner. We talk about America. "When the Americans first

came," they say, "we were all so happy. We thought
it was the end of fascism. But a fascist still commands the naval base. And the fascists still give
orders in the arsenal. We workers could get your
ship out a lot sooner, but they tell us there's no
hurry and the longer we take, the more money there
will be in it for us."

* * *

The people are so jammed against the doors of
the big hall that we, who are the hosts, have to make
up a flying wedge to crash through. Bruce, our
Negro bos'n, spearheads the drive. We have got to
get in there to welcome people. Inside, our French
friends, the trade-union leaders who are giving the
dance with us, rush up and grab our hands. ("Are
you sure these people won't object to mixing the
races?" the Army Special Services officer had asked
the Captain and me when we applied for permission
to use the hall.)

Our friends tell us there hasn't been such a gala
turnout in town since the beginning of the war. Why
haven't the Americans done something like this before, to show they really mean what they say about
unity with their allies?

The place is already packed with people—girls
in their pitiful war-best (most of these people were
bombed out and lost everything): French sailors
with the red pompons on their caps, and their blue
collars; British soldiers; American sailors and

GI's; French workingmen in their patched and shiny suits. On the stage are two orchestras, one French and one a hot band from a Negro anti-aircraft outfit. Back of them are the massed flags of the United Nations, and a big banner we made out of a sheet aboard ship: NATIONAL MARITIME UNION OF AMERICA, CIO.

Dancing has begun and the Captain and I sit down to watch. The Army Special Services officer rushes up to us, enraged and frightened. The dance must be stopped at once; everybody must go home.

"Why?" we ask.

"Too many people," he screams. "We might have a riot."

"But why?" we ask again. "Everybody is orderly. Everybody is having a fine time. If you tried to stop them now, you really would have a riot." We tell him we believe the dance will help to cement good relations with the French.

"I know these French," he says. "They aren't real French. They're mongrels and they hate us. We don't want to have anything to do with them. If I'd known what kind of a dance you were planning, I never would have let you have the hall. I thought you just wanted to ask a few of your special friends."

So he has the door shut, with at least a thousand people outside still trying to get in. But the dance goes on, with easily two thousand inside. Then the MP's appear and the SP's, dozens of them. One

MP Major with a pistol lurches up and down, looking as if he wants to use it. They had found him in his hangout at the Officers' Bar, already pretty far gone. I ask him what trouble he is looking for, and he says, "Too many people," so I explain to him that democracy means people, and there can't be too many. He looks about ready to pull that pistol, so I move on. Somebody says there is a company of troops drawn up outside, ready to break up the affair. This turns out to be only a rumor, or a threat from the drunken major. The closest thing to trouble is when a couple of American lieutenants ask two French women, in the presence of their husbands, to sleep with them that night. This gets handled quietly, by the French and us, while the MP's idly swing their clubs along the walls.

The time comes for speeches. Captain Mulzac gets up in front of the massed flags and the NMU banner and tells everybody in his simple English that this is the kind of thing the American people really stand for, the getting together of the common people all over the world, and they must believe him no matter what they see that would lead them to think something else. Then he announces that the crew of the SS Booker T. Washington is giving one hundreed dollars—five thousands francs—to the French Resistance Movement. Though they haven't understood, the French applaud with huge enthusiasm; and when what he has said is translated to them, the place rocks.

CHAPTER FIFTEEN

Mangiare

THE ITALIAN COAST is close to starboard, blue misty cliffs studded with golden houses. Lieutenant Joe hands me a letter, signed by all the officers in the crack combat outfit (white) we have had aboard for the past week and are about to deliver to the front. "We are unanimous," it reads, "in the realization of our good fortune to have been placed aboard the Booker T. Washington. Many miles we have sailed the seas on other ships, but never before has such good fellowship been shown." Heading the signers is the Southern Colonel in command.

In the dissembling distance, the big port looks like the familiar postcard, but, once inside the mole, we see what's happened. Blasted ships careened at the docksides, stacks and masts sticking up from the water, smashed docks and warehouses, gutted smokeless factories, broken concrete, twisted cranes and bridges, mile upon mile of many-storied workers' tenements, grim enough formerly, now utterly tenantless, blackened stone shells with beds and chairs spilling down from collapsed floor to floor.

A huge barbed wire barricade walls all this area off. Far in the heart of the stony city the stark ribs of what was once a big dome thrust up.

They moor us stern to a half-sunken hulk. It is cold and the wind blows across the wasted acres of docks, sweeping up great clouds of rubble dust. Lines of starred trucks and tanks are moving in the scene and loaded DUKW's swim in from the ships and roll up a ramp to scoot off on their wheels. Hundreds of Italian prisoners, with PW on the backs of their dungaree jackets, work among the mountainous ruins, along with other hundreds of ragged civilians with wheelbarrows.

Some boys come out of a dockside shanty and clamber across the half-sunken hulk to beg cigarettes from the crew on the stern lines. One of them has his feet wrapped in rags. Another wears a man's suit coat so big for him it hangs down to the tops of the GI shoes which some soldier threw away and which this boy now clumps in very carefully to keep from stepping out of them. The boys get their cigarettes and start yelling the usual words foreign kids pick up from us. Their sisters, all aged sixteen, the boys say, are ready to entertain us at such and such an address. The fee will be only thirty five lire. (The exchange rate is one hundred lire to the dollar.)

It has been hardly two weeks since the Nazis were driven out of here. They are only thirty miles away and their bombers pay frequent visits. Before we can even get our troops off, or our explosive cargo, they come over, late at night. The sky is alive with tracer fire and explosions until the acrid smokescreen blots out all but the noise. We pick out the drone of a bomber flying low and a golden flare bursts into light directly over our decks, floating down. We can hear the bomber droning back for the kill. But the flare burns or is shot out in mid-air and the bomb drops wide, smashing down a couple of docks away. The next morning they take our troops off in a lighter and move us to a dock where our explosives are discharged.

When we go ashore at last we learn that it is forbidden to take any food through the gate. The MP's frisk the seamen, and confiscate even sandwiches and chocolate bars intended for their own consumption on a day's expedition. The same rule against feeding the Italians applies aboard ship, where Italian stevedores are unloading us. Many of them are boys of fourteen or fifteen. An MP catches one of these kids gorging himself on spoiled sausages our cooks have thrown in the garbage can. The MP's club cracks down on the kid's skull. One night another kid tries to make off with some C rations from a huge pile on the dock. An MP yells at him to halt but the kid runs. When the heavy slug hits him, he jumps like a rabbit and falls stone-dead.

Only on the heights among the villas and modernistic apartment buildings do the people not beg. Here they pass you with cold faces, well-dressed people, women in fur coats and silk stockings, with male escorts to match, often Italian officers with shiny boots or Navy gold-braid. You even see them stepping into and out of sleek, low-swung Bugattis with Allied Military Government stickers on their windshields. Up here you see no writing on the walls viva-ing the Allies but rather the proclamations of the Nazi military governor still in place.

Down below in the clammy stinking alleys that climb by stairs between great stone cliffs of workers' tenements, the populace besieges you. Sometimes they just ask: for chewing gum, "caramelli," chocolate, money. Or maybe they want to sell something: a bottle labeled "champagne," a spaghetti dinner. A tiny girl, just eyes in a shawl down to her heels, offers herself to me. Troops of boys tag at your heels, wanting to take you to their "sisters." Along the walls are shrines with plaster saints whose paint has faded. Every second ground-floor has blossomed out as a black-market restaurant and bar, and you can see the GI's eating and drinking around the family table. A big gaudy church has been hit by a bomb. The sky shows through above the transept, and the gilt of the cherub-encrusted high altar is bleared with rubble dust. A few ragged old women are kneeling among the columns of rich, varicolored stone.

Blockbusters have fallen all through here, and from the tumbled ruins comes the nauseous whiff of death where corpses still lie beneath the tons of

stone. But on the walls you read "Viva Gli Alleati"
and Mussolini's stenciled picture is everywhere
smeared out with black paint. Also you can read,
now and again, DEATH TO FASCISM. OUT WITH BADO-
GLIO. OUT WITH THE KING. LONG LIVE COMMUNISM.
These lines of women with sunken eyes and shawls
over worn-out shoddy dresses, shuffling in their
wrecks of shoes, are waiting to buy something—a
little bread, a little oil on ration tickets. To live, it
is necessary to supplement this on the black market
where a loaf of bread or a pound of spaghetti costs
a day's pay, a pound of meat or cheese two days'
pay and a quart of oil three days' pay. Assuming of
course that one is getting paid by the Americans,
working on the docks, clearing rubble from the
streets. All the factories are in ruins. How many
are out of work, nobody even tries to guess.

More than a year later we come back, bringing
cargo and Italian soldiers from Africa, who have
been war prisoners since the Tunisian campaign
twenty months ago. Now they are all dressed up in
new American uniforms with Italian insignia.
They will be put into the line against the Nazis.
Their officers huddle aside in a little group on the
forward deck, not speaking to the men except to
order them to do something which is then half-done.
The officers make the men bring them their breakfast in bed down below until we find out and put a
stop to it.

Some of the Italian-Americans in our crew get

talking to the soldiers. They say they are willing to
fight the Nazis and help to run them out of Italy.
But they will not, they say, fight under the *"signorine"*—the young ladies—meaning their officers.
Under American officers or even British officers,
yes. But not under their own, who are strictly no
good. In Tunisia the *"signorine"* were the first to
run away. They will run away again or go over to
the Germans. They are still fascists in their hearts,
these officers. How can a man risk his life in battle
against fascism behind such leadership?

Among the Italians are ten stowaways who appeared after the ship sailed from Africa, having
slipped aboard among the stevedores and hidden in
a hold full of automobile tires. All ten were prisoners taken by us but turned over to the French. All
but one have been working on the farms of French
colonials. Their stories are virtually the same: they
were beaten just like the Arabs who worked alongside them from dawn to dusk; fed only on peas and
beans; given brackish water to drink; straw to sleep
on in some shed or wellhouse; they watched comrades die of typhoid and dysentery; they listened to
threats of how much worse it would go for them
once the Americans got out and French colonials
could deal with them as Italians really deserved.
The stowaways have but one fear: of being turned
over to the French authorities. They are vastly relieved when they learn that they will be sent instead
to the front.

The first these returning soldiers see of their people is on a blustery afternoon when the convoy passes in a single column through a narrow waterway. Here, lined up for at least a mile athwart the convoy's course are hundreds of small boats which have put out from an Italian city on the shore. They are manned by boys, most of them barefooted despite the icy wind and the water shipped from the wakes of the big vessels passing. You can see how red and cold are their feet and hands. Many have small American flags like the ones children carry in fourth of July parades at home. As the big ships slide by their crazily rocking boats, they stretch out poles with nets on the end. *"Mangiare!"* they are shouting, *"Mangiare!"*

But this is such an old story now that nobody does anything about it, and so far as I can tell not a scrap of food is flung to the boats from any one of the ships in the mighty line. The Italian soldiers on their way to fight Nazis line the rail and silently watch the small boats, the barefoot boys screaming for something to eat, fall behind on the cold sea against the snowy Italian mountains from which the wind is blowing.

CHAPTER SIXTEEN

Jim Crow Rest Camp

THE REST CAMP is a villa on a cliff above the sea where Negro fliers and combat officers get ten-day leaves to come back to normal. The heart of the place is a cozy bar, well-stocked with cognac, strega, cherry brandy, vermouth, and gin. The bar specialty is called "Strange Fruit" and consists of one jigger each of the five liquors in stock, with cocoa for the mix. A few of these over an evening will successfully knock out a man's memories.

Off the bar is a big room, with a juke box and a floor for dancing, card tables and a moth-eaten pool table. A big gasoline stove roars in the center. Across the hall is a dining room, where good food is served, and across the street the dormitory, a remodeled apartment house. Better quarters couldn't be provided, only the Jim Crow flavor makes us from the Booker T. Washington somewhat ill at ease, as cordially as we are received.

These young officers from a famous pursuit squadron and an equally famous infantry division are as meticulously uniformed as the officers of the white combat outfits we have had aboard. Across their battle jackets they wear just as many ribbons, the same ribbons, studded with oak leaf clusters and stars. When we talk with them, we find them as well-educated and informed and possibly more aware of the great issues and meanings of this war. The only difference is the skin color and that is what disturbs us, coming back into our consciousness after the months on the Booker T. Washington where you pay no more attention to that particular than to the color of a man's eyes, the shape of his nose or the quality of his voice. But how conscious they are of their color. How conscious the Army has kept them of it! We sense it as an obstacle to full communication, almost like a foreign language, even those from our ship who share their color.

But around the bar the reserve melts slowly away and honest, easy talk wells up. Under it all is the familiar note of deep resentment which you can hear from any Negro soldiers in our Army, if he trusts you with his real feelings. He may be a decorated hero whose picture has been in all the Negro papers and his name perhaps in some of the white ones. Or he may be an ordinary stevedore in a port battalion. His resentment will seldom be personal and he will often laugh uproariously over the ludicrous hypocrisy of the practices by which he has been personally victimized. But he is uniformly bitter over the treatment accorded his race in this war. Hardships and dangers are not the themes of his beefs, which, in all their complexity, can be summed up as a many-voiced protest against Jim Crow.

The man who on dozens of missions flew escort to the white crews in the bombers and fought off Nazis over Munich and Vienna, shepherding his bombers safely back, is not reconciled to his segregated rest-camp, equal though it may be in its accommodations to the one offered the white officers of the bombers. And the man who has stormed an enemy mountain position without artillery support and then held it for terrible days and nights side by side with a white officer, with whom he shared his rations, will never accept the iron precept that, except under field conditions, the two of them must not eat together. The task of making the Negro satisfied with Jim Crow is a hopeless one, more difficult of attainment each day that our authorities battle to accomplish it against the tide of world history and common human aspiration. On our ship we know how frail the barriers of prejudice prove to be when we live, work, and fight together. Jim Crow is a straw man. It's high time he was demolished. Nor is it too late for the services to tackle the job of demolition during this war. The other policy has dismally failed, with catastrophic results to our own morale and to American prestige in the countries where we have imported this straw-man fetish of ours. What we need are mixed Army units, mixed Navy ships, and I mean mixed as the Booker T. Washington is mixed; from the topside down through the galley to the engine room below, mixed in every fo'c'sle, in every mess-room. And this should be done not on an experimental but a broad basis.

It will work out just as the Booker T. Washington has worked out; provided only that those in charge try as honestly to make it succeed as they have been trying to make Jim Crow work.

I get to know a man at the rest camp who could be a powerful leader in such a program, a Negro colonel who has just been relieved from his command of a combat regiment, a man with a shining record in the last war and this one, a man who began his service as an enlisted cavalryman at the time of the Mexican border trouble and fought his way through sheer indomitable quality to a rank held by very few men of his race. He is being sent home for medical reasons, his blood pressure having reached a point considered dangerous for a man in a combat post. He is sad at leaving his regiment, of which he is very proud, having been with it first as executive and then as commanding officer since its activation in 1940. But he knows it is a solidly built organization and will not fall apart at his leaving. What he seems most proud of is how well his men behave toward the civilian populations among whom they have been quartered. Recently they

served as the garrison of a small Italian city near
the front. When they took over from the white outfit, they found the town plastered with off-limits
signs. The MP's had been thick there. The Negro
colonel took down all the off-limits signs. He de-
tailed a lieutenant as provost-marshal and gave him
one sergeant as MP. He told the lieutenant his
primary responsibility was to win the trust of the
Italian people and the shortest cut to that end
was to learn their language thoroughly. Within a
month the lieutenant could converse with the people. The Colonel had no trouble, either with the
Italians or with his own men. When the regiment
was withdrawn, the whole town mourned their going and the town council sent a long resolution to
the Colonel, telling him that he and his men made
them honor and love America as never before.

CHAPTER SEVENTEEN

Liberty Party

WHILE WE'RE BUILDING UP
for the Italian invasion, this North African port is
just about our biggest. The cramped harbor is solid
with Liberties, troop ships and LST's. Warships

crowd the naval base, American and British and French, from patrol craft up to battle-wagons, some of these among the best-known in the business.

Allied sailors and troops surge through the streets of the city. Here are not only the men from the armada bristling on the blue below the sunset-colored cliffs but also GI's from a dozen nearby camps, Senegalese and Goums and fezzed Algerians in training, French officers in resplendent caps, Foreign Legionnaires, British armored force men in black berets like Monty's. You see everybody in this thing, all looking for a good time before they get back into it.

Romance ought to lurk, they figure in their milling dozens, down these curving stone stairs, hollowed by slippered feet through centuries, debouching on a cobbled alley twisting out of sight between grilled houses. So down they go and, rounding the turn, encounter not romance but the waiting white-helmeted MP's.

We make that port after tense weeks at sea. The subs are running thick outside and ganged up with torpedo planes on the Persian Gulf wing of our convoy, carrying supplies for Russia. The whole calm sea was shaken with explosions while tracers looped gold across the twilight. The guys are glad to get land under their feet again after this, and, as soon as liberty is granted, troop ashore in a bantering mob. Since our ship is the SS Booker T. Washington, naturally they go altogether, whites mixed up with Negroes. Coming to the curving stone stairs, they stream down, their loud and happy voices echoing in the narrow defile between the houses. At the bottom, they follow the cobbled alley around the enticing bend.

The MP's bring seventeen of them back aboard in a truck, and a mass trial is held in the Captain's quarters, with an MP Major as the judge. Captain Mulzac doesn't like it.

"What were they doing wrong?" he demands to know.

"They were picked up in the Casbah, in the Arab quarter," the MP Major says.

"What's wrong with their going in the Casbah?" the Captain asks.

"It's off limits," the Major says. "All the Casbah is off limits to American and British forces."

"Why is it off limits?" the Captain persists.

"They might get robbed," the Major says. "They might catch something. They might eat an un-cooked vegetable."

"You mean they might buy something from the Arabs," the Captain says. "They might not spend all their money with the French."

Souvenirs like slippers with turned-up toes, and leather cigarette cases, and silver rings, cost a good deal less in the Casbah shops than in those of the French boulevards. The Captain knew all these ports in pre-war days, when there were no off-limits. He doesn't take any stock in the official theory that

the Arabs have it in for Americans and will rob or
knife you if they get the chance. When you're hitch-
hiking out to the naval base, an Arab will pick you
up in his jalopy truck or car before a Frenchman
will in his lend-lease jeep. " 'Mericans good!" all
the Arab kids call after you in the streets.

The mass trial commences and each of the seventeen men testifies that he didn't see any off-limits
sign. The MP squad had let them walk right on
into the Casbah, had just stood there without warning them or anything and, once they were well inside, pounced. The MP's were tough about it, too,
threatening to use their clubs if the guys wouldn't
come along. No self-respecting white man, an MP
said, would run around ashore with "niggers." The
guys all have the idea that this is the main reason
they were picked up, and the MP Major can't
change their minds. When he pronounces sentences
of a $25 fine apiece on the seventeen men, somebody
whispers, "the son of a bitch!" The MP Major has
no luck trying to find the culprit, though he warns
that this is one of the gravest offenses under the
military law to which we are subject, flagrant dis-
respect to an officer of the United States in the
course of doing his duty, or words to that effect.
Apparently the MP Major is the only one in the
room who heard the whisper. Even Captain Mulzac didn't.

Each of the seventeen men signs the log-book for
$25 and the Captain pays over $425 in cold cash to

the MP Major, remarking as he does so that the
Arabs, granting they were out to rob our guys,
couldn't have done so good a job.

Later that evening Sparks and Tres come aboard
together. Sparks is black and Tres is white. They
had been with the crowd in the Casbah but had
ducked into an archway when the MP's closed in.
It opened on another alley, pitch-black, and they
ran like hell. Turning the next corner, they saw a
family in a ground-floor window all sitting around
a table under the light. Sparks and Tres ran right
in and pulled up chairs. Tres yanked a bottle of
wine from under his coat and slammed it down on
the table. The family turned out to be anti-fascist
Spanish refugees who lived in the Casbah because
the Arabs were friendly and the rent was low. On
the wall of the room were pictures of Roosevelt,
Churchill, and Stalin. Tres opened the wine and
they passed the bottle around the table, everybody
including the Spaniard and his wife and their two
kids taking swigs from it, first to Roosevelt, then to
Churchill and then to Stalin. The MP's never did
catch Sparks and Tres.

The Red Cross has two clubs in town, one for
whites and one for Negroes, though the Red Cross
says not. It is just that one club has an all-white
staff and the other an all-Negro staff. If a Negro
happens into the club with the all-white staff,
which he is likely to do since it is in the center of

town while the other is way to hell out, one of the all-white staff may suggest to him that he will feel more at home in the club with the all-Negro staff, and give him polite directions regarding the best corner to stand on to thumb a ride out. Whites who blunder into the club with the all-Negro staff are apt to stay, even to come back again, for the snack bar is the best in town. At their dances, though, the only whites present are the girls. They are a group assembled by the Red Cross and their mothers sit around the walls benignly watching their offsprings being taught how to jitterbug by the colored soldiers, while a Negro GI band plays jump after jump. Added to these girls are others brought in by the boys, just French and Spanish girls they happened to meet. But at one dance several of the Negro boys show up with Arab girls.

Consternation grips the benign mothers on the sidelines. They have no objection to their daughters dancing and otherwise associating with the brown Americans ("who are so much more *gentils* than the white ones, less disorderly and more considerate") but they draw the line at their sharing the same dance floor with native girls. Getting together, the outraged mothers decide on a common course of action, and present an ultimatum to the Red Cross club management: the Arab girls must be ejected immediately or they will take their daughters home, never to return. Soon the French police arrive, the Arab girls are collared and marched off, and the white girls go on happily jitterbugging with the brown Americans.

We come back to that port nearly two years later. Now it is only a convoy rendezvous. The war has swept past it. They have closed up the Red Cross club with the all-Negro staff. The other one is still open, serving both races. We are out at the naval base, waiting for convoy. Chiquita Lonewolf, a Red Cross worker held over from the all-Negro staff though as her name shows she is an older American than those who draw the color line, comes aboard to see that we have a good Christmas. Chiquita takes us up the mountainside for Christmas trees, into the pine groves. And she rounds up decorations, icicles and stars and streamers. They are having a pre-Christmas dance, Chiquita says, at the Red Cross club, and they want us to come. A poster goes up, on the ship's bulletin board, inviting everybody. We are to be the honored guests, and the fellows put on their best. Things like this mean a lot, at Christmas time, and so far from home.

Chiquita sends a truck for us, all the way out to the naval base, and nearly everybody piles on, officers and men. But when we reach the club, there's a hitch. The MP's stop the white guys at the door.

"This is Negro night," they say. "No whites allowed."

"But we're all from the Booker T. Washington. We're shipmates."

"Can't help that. The white guys can't come in. It's orders."

By this time Captain Mulzac is asking the questions. "Whose orders?" he wants to know.

"The Army doesn't want us to mix the races," says the Red Cross club director who has come up. "The Army doesn't want any fights or anything like that. So we have white nights and colored nights. This is a colored night, and only colored can come inside and dance."

"But the girls are white," the Captain says. "The girls are the same girls every night."

"Oh yes," the Red Cross man says. "That's why we have to keep the races separate. We might have trouble if we had white and colored breaking in on the same girls."

"We won't come in here," Captain Mulzac says, speaking for all the Negroes off the Booker T. Washington. "Not a single one of us will come inside a place where we all can't."

It's Christmas eve. The rule is that you can't bring liquor into the port area. But nearly everybody wants some cheer for Christmas. A lot of the guys buy cognac or wine up in town to bring aboard ship. That's the way it is on all the ships in the harbor.

Four of our guys are coming back aboard together this Christmas eve. Brownie is white, and he has three bottles of cognac under his coat. Mickey, a Negro, has one bottle. Sam, the Deck Engineer, and Second Sparks, both Negroes, have no bottles. They are both serious guys with tough fights behind them, to get where they are, Sam a chief petty officer and Second Sparks wearing a warrant officer's stripe. Neither of them will take a chance on marring their perfect conduct records, just for a little Christmas cheer.

Brownie, the white man, is first through the gate. The MP's frisk him and find all three bottles. They take two of them and let him pass on through with one. They frisk Mickey next.

"What you doing, boy," the sergeant asks him, "with this bottle?"

When Mickey doesn't say anything, Second Sparks speaks up. "You just let a guy through with one bottle," he says. Sam doesn't say anything, but that doesn't keep him from being arrested along with Mickey and Second Sparks. An MP marches the three Negroes to the Provost Marshal's inside the gate, keeping his 45 trained on their backs and threatening to use it unless they step livelier.

At the Provost Marshal's, the lounging MP's have some fun with the three Negroes, like at the police station back home in Georgia. "You've disgraced your uniforms," they say to Second Sparks and Sam. "We oughta rip 'em off a you." The three are booked for attempting to enter the port area with three bottles of liquor—Mickey's one and the two previously confiscated from the white guy, Brownie. They are released but told to appear for trial at 0900 Christmas morning. I appear with them, as defense counsel, and bring along Brownie as a material witness. He is pretty sore when he hears that his colored shipmates have taken the rap for his two bottles, and insists on coming.

"What a night," the MP corporal on duty as clerk of court says. "What a head I've got." All the MP's look as if they'd put in a tough Christmas eve, disposing of all that evidence. Even the Acting Provost Marshal does, a lieutenant from Texas, who takes me into a back room to talk things over when he learns I'm there to defend the Negroes. The whole thing can be quashed if the guys will just plead guilty and accept seven days' restriction to the ship, which won't matter since we're sailing in a couple of days anyway. I consult my clients outside and go back in to tell him that they won't plead guilty and they demand courts-martial. He calls in a Coast Guard lieutenant from the Merchant Marine Hearing Unit next door. He says the men, for their own good, should plead guilty.

"But they aren't guilty," I say. "They didn't have three bottles. One of them had one bottle. The other two didn't have any. They got credit for two bottles taken off a white guy, who passed through the gate with another and wasn't even arrested."

"OK," the Provost Marshal says, "they want courts-martial and they're going to get them. You want to start something, but you can be damn sure we'll finish it and finish it right."

"When you say 'finish it right,' you better mean 'finish it justly,'" I say, "or it still won't be finished."

"Keep a civil tongue in your head, Purser," the Coast Guard lieutenant tells me, "or you'll be in this too. What business is it of yours anyway?"

The three Negroes are never court-martialed and Brownie gets no chance to testify.

George, the Negro mess-boy in the officers' saloon, comes back aboard all excited. He has just met a swell guy in a bar uptown who's coming down tomorrow with a jeep and take whoever wants to go to a city in the interior where there aren't any MP's and you can have a time. The guy is white, but he's very democratic and used to belong to the NMU, back in the early days. He wears an Army officer's uniform, without rank insignia, and is some sort of intelligence agent, checking up on civilians.

"How did he happen to pick up with you, George?" Alex asks him.

"Oh, he knows all about the Booker T. Washington," George says. "He's an old-time union man."

"I ought to know him then," Alex says. "Did he tell you his name?"

"No," George says, "he didn't."

But when Louis gets back from uptown he takes Alex aside. He asks him if he remembers a certain guy, naming him.

"You mean the phony?" Alex says. "You mean the labor spy who tried to wreck the union?"

"He's in town," Louis says. "He's in uniform but he's up to something. I saw him in a bar, buying George drinks, the mess-boy George."

That night we have a special ship's meeting. Alex gets up and tells about the phony, how he worked his way high up into the union and, when he got there, tried to split it and turn the white guys against the Negroes. He tells how the phony and his gang raided union headquarters with baseball bats, insulted the girls who worked there, and beat up the Negroes they caught. He tells how the union got the goods on the phony, proving he was on the payroll of a notorious labor spy outfit, and expelled him after trial. He tells how the phony then got inside another union and tried to wreck it.

George the mess-boy says the phony told him he was all for the Booker T. Washington because he was against any kind of discrimination.

"You see me," Captain Mulzac says, getting up, "I'm one of the Negroes his gang beat up with baseball bats, trying to run us out of the union."

Before the meeting ends, we plan a reception for the phony, when he comes aboard tomorrow to take George and his friends on the jeep expedition to the city where there aren't any MP's.

At the appointed hour, the phony pulls up in his jeep and steps on the deckside where there's a crowd of Nazi prisoners messing around. They sometimes sweep a little or scrape a few barnacles off a ship's side in drydock, while the Arabs do the heavy work. Mostly they lean on their brooms or scrapers and haggle for cigarettes and food. They have quite an industry out in their camp, making bogus Nazi medals out of scrap aluminum, which they trade to the Americans.

The phony hops out of his jeep and the Nazis flock around him, grinning and clicking their heels. He grins back and says something pleasant. Then he comes swinging up the gangway, very dapper in his uniform without rank insignia but with a gold US on each side of his collar. The minute he hits the after-deck, Louis, who has been hiding just inside the entrance to the starboard alleyway, starts ringing the big dinner bell and the guys come swarming from all over the ship. They encircle the phony on the after-deck, look down on him from the boat deck, but nobody does anything. The phony turns toward the gangway and nobody stops him. He goes down fast and makes for the jeep. The Nazis grin and click their heels. He waves to them and jumps in, starts the engine, turns on a dime, and beats it in a hell of a hurry.

CHAPTER EIGHTEEN

The Day of Glory Has Arrived

ADJUTANT JACQUES MENIER, the warrant officer in charge of the French soldiers we are repatriating to their homeland from Italy, is exactly my age. Checking further on the parallel between us while we share some real American whiskey in my cabin, we discover that we both married our wives in the same year and have had the same number of children—four— three boys and one girl in both cases. They would be aged approximately the same except that all mine are still living.

In May, 1940, Jacques Menier's wife, together with three of his four children, simply disappeared. No trace of them has ever been found. They were in a refugee train that was bombed, he supposes, or a Stuka got them on the road. He has one boy left, in a religious home near Bordeaux, according to word from relatives. Jacques Menier has not been home for almost six years. The fall of France found him serving in French Equatorial Africa. He was an officer over Negro troops in what became the First Battalion of the First Free

French Division. He started with them from Pointe Noire at the Congo's mouth, and made the gigantic trek up through the jungles and across the whole Sahara to the Nile, which they descended to join the British forces in Egypt in 1941. They fought through the whole terrible desert campaign. There are no soldiers to equal the Negro troops he commanded, Jacques Menier says. He wonders whether we Americans hate the Nazis enough, whether we know the kind of enemy we're up against. The Boches, he says, mined not only their dead. "Once I came on an Austrian whose guts were spilling out but he was still alive. He knew French, this Austrian. And when I came up to help him he screamed at me not to touch him, that there was a mine right under his back, which his retreating comrades had put there. We left him to die in the desert."

Jacques Menier was in on the Italian invasion and fought all the long way up the peninsula, but when his division went on to capture Toulon in the liberation of Southern France, he was left behind in the hospital. The troops under his command aboard ship are French war prisoners released by the Russians in their drive through Rumania, Hungary, and Poland. They were flown to Italy, and we are taking them the rest of the way home. Nearly five years they have been exiled. They cluster on the deck and silently watch for a long time, though the cold mistral is blowing, when the

Maritime Alps show their snowy crests over the horizon.

This is not the France I left in 1928—the easy, gracious land of good food and wine, of gemlike Romanesque churches reached by bicycle along a curving, hedged-in lane. I would not know it. Rubble dust. Ruins of buildings, still death-smelling from the corpses underneath. Hunger. Gaunt, threadbare people. Shops with empty shelves. The shipload of fish that was known to arrive yesterday has been discharged, but there is no fish in the shops where the queued people stand. Like everything else, the fish has found its way to the black market, where it is sold at prices even the Americans cannot afford to pay.

Last night all the stevedores in the port struck for several hours. It started on the dock by our ship. An American MP shot a stevedore. One story is that the stevedore was trying to steal a box of rations. Another is that the MP was drunk. Yet another is that the pile of boxes, on which the MP was standing, slipped under him and his rifle went off by accident.

"Ought to shoot them all down like dogs," said an American Navy boy standing at our gangway.

George Alafousas, the First Assistant, and I walked up the docks after the shooting. The stevedores had stopped work on all the ships and had gathered in great angry clusters on the docksides. *"Les Américains,"* we could hear them hissing.

"Whatever the truth of it," the French union official tells us next day, "people will go on talking and the worst will be believed, because of all the other things that have happened."

The union official has only one shirt, fantastically ragged. It is absolutely impossible to get a shirt in the city, he says. One of us offers him an old shirt. He declines, with profuse thanks, saying that he could not possibly accept it.

"It is military," he says. "The MP's would take it away from me at the gate."

"But if you put it on and wear it?"

"That would make no difference," he says. "They would strip it off my back. My brother is also a stevedore. An American soldier saw how broken his shoes were and took pity on him. It is not possible to get shoes here. The soldier gave an old pair of his own shoes to my brother, who then threw away his broken ones. He did not know that it was against the rules. At the gate, the American MP's asked him where he'd got the military shoes. When he told them, they took him to jail. They kept him there all night, and in the morning they tried him and revoked his work permit for eight days. Then they made him take his shoes off. He had to walk home six kilometers without shoes, in the cold and rain. All he has now are some old canvas ones. And losing a week's work meant that my brother's family suffered very much. Even if one works every possible day, it is difficult to live."

Coming back from our official rounds at port headquarters in the city, the Captain and I are stopped by what seems a parade. At the head is a huge red flag with the hammer and sickle and "CCCP"—the Russian characters for USSR—inscribed on it. Behind the banner, men are swinging along beautifully in step, though they are wearing all sorts of ragged civilian clothes and bits and pieces of uniforms. A few have on red-starred caps. A bystander tells us that these are Russian soldiers, released prisoners of the Germans, who are working on the docks while waiting to be sent home. Suddenly they break into a deep marching song. Singing it, they wheel out of sight behind the broken slabs of a demolished building, but their banner and their song have left a brightness on the gray, rainy air.

I buy all the French newspapers. Every one of them gives the main play to the British intervention in Greece and, though their political colorations are diverse, they are united in denouncing it. A few days later, de Gaulle's trip to Moscow and the conclusion of the Franco-Soviet pact have the top spot. Again, all the papers are united, this time in common acclaim.

The Yugoslav consul, Lazar Latinovic, was until recently a major in Tito's army. He has no living relatives. The last to go were his mother and father. To punish them for having a Partisan son, the

Germans locked them in their home in Belgrade, then set it afire. Women in cafés make flattering remarks about Major Latinovic as they brush by, for he is tremendously tall and fiery-looking. But the fire in him burns not for them and he pays them no mind. He drinks only an occasional vermouth or glass of wine, and does not smoke at all. Major Latinovic is an honored guest for dinner aboard our ship, of which he knows already because of what we did for his people on a previous trip.

Not that it was much—cigarettes, candy, some old clothing for a British-administered Yugoslav hospital on the Italian Adriatic coast. Hospital was hardly the right word for this place. In it were women and children mostly, as well as some wounded, evacuated from the parts of Dalmatia which the Nazis had reconquered. The people had little clothing. The children had no shoes. There were few physicians and no medicines. The children were dying in masses from measles, which cut them down in their condition as if it were a plague. The sick slept on concrete floors, with little covering. Yet because we gave them a little donation, hardly a drop in the bucket of their need, they invited us to be their guests, and a crowd from the ship went out on a truck. They put on an anti-fascist play for us with a Hitler so realistic that one of our boys, who had got slightly gassed up, had to be restrained from going up on the stage after him.

Major Latinovic is now trying to round up all the Yugoslav prisoners in France and get them home again, where they are needed to fight Nazis. There are perhaps as many as twenty thousand of these. But the British and American authorities have ruled that only Yugoslav soldiers captured by the Nazis prior to May 31, 1941, are entitled to the treatment accorded Allied prisoners of war. That means only the soldiers of the Royal Yugoslav army who were captured in the initial Nazi blitz. All of Tito's men who fell into Nazi hands during the long years of bitter struggle in the mountains, and were transported to work camps in France, are classified as "displaced persons." Thousands of them are still locked up in the same camps with Nazis captured by the Allies. Repatriation is going quite slowly at the moment, for the Americans say that the reception camps in Italy, where the Yugoslavs are held awaiting air transport home, are overloaded. Even greater numbers of Russians are backed up waiting, including the column I saw marching on the street.

"How do we know who this man is?" the American security officer asks when we come back to that port again and I request a second pass for Major Latinovic to come aboard ship.

"He has his passport and official identity card," I say. "His office is in a big villa with a sign over the door saying that it is the Yugoslavian Consulate. He is the representative of an Allied power and a friend of ours. We want to entertain him and hear what he has to say, so we can take the story home to the United States. Our people of Yugoslav descent would like to hear it. So would all the Americans who want to help Yugoslavia for what she has done in this war."

The pass is not granted.

I take Major Latinovic to a "Franco-American Revue" at a city theatre. This has been arranged by the Negro officer of the United States Army Special Services. The theatre is filled to capacity with French and American soldiers and their girls, all mixed up, with no segregation according to color or nationality. Though the French singers are good, the American Negroes make the greatest hit, the audience going wild over the hot band and its cavorting GI leader, over the quartet singing "Water Boy" and "Suwannee River." We go away wondering why a lot more of this isn't done. Having fun together is one of the best ways for peoples to come to understand each other.

Before we part, Major Latinovic takes a copy of an article I wrote for a magazine at home on the SS Booker T. Washington. He wants to send it to his country for translation and reprinting, so the Yugoslavs will know more about our ship and about what Americans really mean by their word democracy. And I promise him that, for our part, we will tell the people of America that the people of Yugoslavia, their Allies, are in desperate need of everything—of food, clothing, medicines, doctors, and of help in getting their captured fighters home where they can fight again against the common foe. No people deserve more of us than the Yugoslavs. At least that's what we all think aboard the SS Booker T. Washington, and a group of American P-38 pilots we once transported thought the same thing. They had many comrades living today whom they had given up for lost when they were shot down over Yugoslavia. But they had turned up in Italy months later, having been sheltered by this almost homeless people, fed by this close-to-starving people, and brought through to safety by those who have known no safety since May 31, 1941.

We from the SS Booker T. Washington are the only Americans present at the dance, the first held by the French since the Liberation. Unless, that is, you count the two American MP's in white helmets posted at the door. This pair look unhappy and full of foreboding. "These FFI's," they say, repeating what we have heard so often from other Americans, "are just a bunch of gangsters. There's going to be plenty of trouble." But there is no trouble.

These French soldiers and sailors, these fighters of the Resistance in shabby civilian clothes, these little working girls, look uncertainly at us gold-braided American officers and shrink back, leaving a path for us across the crowded dance floor. But, later, when they learn that we are there as friends, not as police, they mass around us. We are standing on a stairway, looking down at all the young faces. The dancing has stopped and the orchestra is waiting for the signal. A young woman leader gives it. "Now we will sing our song of the French youth for our American comrades." The song is *"Au Devant de la Vie,"* and its chorus goes, "Stand up, my blond, sing to the wind. Stand up, friends. Our country marches toward the rising sun." Then without any further signal, they break into the *"Marseillaise,"* sung with an inconceivable and shattering fervor, its old meaning bursting out of each ringing line, and all the faces below looking as the faces must have looked when that song was first sung, in 1792.

CHAPTER NINETEEN

Nazi Cargo

Up THE GANGWAY they come, the beaten enemy, five hundred Nazi prisoners captured in Italy. Our MP's covering them with tommy-guns down on the dock are big fellows in

combat boots and helmets with goggles pushed up
on them. Any one of the MP's looks capable of
handling any ten of these Nazis, even without his
tommy gun.

We watch the Nazis coming aboard from the
starboard wing of the bridge. Up there are Captain
Mulzac and Chief Mate Cliff Lastic and Lieutenant Jim Youngdale, the senior gunnery officer, and
myself. The Captain has on a white shirt and pants
and a battered pair of Romeo slippers with the
sides slit out to ease his feet. All he wears to let you
know he is anybody aboard is a pressure cap, but
the gold of the insignia and the braid are green
with salt and the khaki cover is daubed with battleship gray paint. The Captain likes to paint out his
own quarters, the chartroom and wheelhouse, because he is a much better hand with a brush than
any of the sailors.

"Supermen!" Cliff Lastic says and laughs his
big rich laugh. The sleeves of his rough slop-chest
shirt are rolled up showing his thick arms, the
tattooing lush blue and red over the deep native
brown of his skin. Long ago he had them done,
when he was a British sailor in the first war, and
one tattoo depicts the Cross of Ages because Cliff,
at that time, was pious. "Wait till they find out
what kind of a ship they're on!"

"Those guys," the Captain says, "I don't see why
they have to send them to the United States. We've
already got too many people like them. We ought

to leave them right here in Africa, build a big camp in the middle of the Sahara desert and put all the Nazis in it."

Jim Youngdale scratches the hair on his chest, an absent-minded habit he has when he is thinking hard about something. Jim seldom wears even a skivy shirt and never puts on any of his Navy officer's insignia except when he's going ashore and has to. For all that he has good discipline in the gun crew, just about the best we've ever had, and the guns stay clean and ready to shoot, any minute, the 20 millimeters, the 3-inch 50's and the big one on the platform aft.

"Maybe you could do something with those birds," Jim says. "They look hungry enough to absorb some education."

"I don't know," I say, for I really don't. "But we ought either to try or else finish them off quick. One or the other."

In single file, the Nazis struggle up the gangway. They haven't much to carry, any of them, but it seems about all they can do to put one foot in front of the other, shod in heavy hobnailed boots. I keep trying to spot the German doctor the Army said we were going to get to take care of all these guys. They look as if they are going to need a lot of attention. They are a sickly bunch. And young. Most of them look more like boy-scouts who got rained on out on their hike than they do like soldiers of a great army. But there are older fellows among them too, with thin crooked noses and bald spots, looking too tired to care about anything any more.

But I don't see anybody who answers to the description of a doctor. One lanky kid comes weaving up with a Red Cross bag on his back. Clearly I am going to have all these guys and their ailments on my hands, plus the Army escort guard, though they don't look as if they could have anything the matter with them beyond maybe athlete's foot. The last Nazi comes aboard and with a tommy-gun at his back clumps down the companionway to the 'tweendecks quarters, filled solid with five-decker bunks. The clusters of watchers on the forward deck and perched on the masts break up, the Navy boys in their dungarees looking so enormously fitter than the Nazi boys their age. John Skerlick, our Bos'n this trip, moves on from where he has been posed with arms akimbo, swarthy and black-bearded, the Slav avenger with heavy sunburned torso. Able Seaman Junius comes down from the masthead where he had seemed like some jungle warrior about to spring, the rich African sunlight burnishing his black muscle-rippling hide.

Over the fantastic city with its minarets of ancient mosques and futuristic outlines of *confort-moderne* apartments the sun from the west throws its enveloping light. There in that sharp masonry cluster of gold is the tasteful dwelling of Monsieur Amadée, overlord of the *poules de luxe* and boss of the black market. There also in the ghetto of the Medina is the one-room home of twelve-year-old Ibrahim who speaks five languages and guides American officers to the hang-outs of M. Amadée's forty dollar *poules*. There under the fly-swarming guts of sheep at the portal, sits Ibrahim's father, the butcher with the trachoma eyes, while lined up in the cobbled alley the hungry people shove closer and closer to the stinking food.

The French pilot comes aboard in his beret, and we cast off forward and aft. The tug warps us out from the dock where in the shade of warehouses the ragged Arab stevedores are eating watermelons. After the war, the Arabs solemnly tell you, they are all coming to the United States to live, where a man earns a hundred francs—two dollars!—a day and get out of this country which the French have taken away from them. Before the war, the French paid them only three francs a day. The Americans pay them forty francs a day—eighty cents. The French employers are very sore about this. "An Arab," M. Amadée will tell you, "has a low standard of living. His needs are simple. If you pay him in a day what he used to earn in a week, he will work only one day a week. The Arab is a child. To get work out of him, you must pay him the least possible. It is for his own good, and for the upbuilding of the country."

Once the Arabs were discharging us and got into a consignment of canned milk in the cargo. They just sat down where they were in the hold, those emaciated Arabs, and drank down that milk by the case. Probably they had never tasted cow's milk before in all their lives. Then they were sick all over the hold. Another day our black gang dug out all their old clothes to give the Arabs. The Arabs would pay ten days' earnings for a pair of old dungarees, they were that naked. But the black gang got charitable and threw down their oil-soaked pants and busted-up shoes to them for nothing. The Arabs fought and clawed each other for them all over the deck.

We're out in the stream now and the engines begin turning over, the deep thump that brings a ship alive and keeps the rhythm of the long sea-borne days. Up on the bridge the sailors unlash the name boards on each side, BOOKER T. WASHINGTON, and stow them. Now we're just another Liberty, flying a convoy number. I wonder what the Nazis thought reading our name-board as they came up the gangway, and whether BOOKER T. WASHINGTON registered anything in their minds?

Mike Sala is the utility man who makes up our bunks every morning. Cliff Lastic at the head of the passageway will be just about going to sleep after coming off his 4-to-8 watch when Mike hits my door on his rounds. "Mister Beech," he almost shouts, " 'scuse but I been thinking. . . ." And Cliff up the passageway as well as myself will learn of

Mike's indignation with Prime Minister Churchill for trying to keep Italy saddled with the monarchy. Before going to sea, Mike wrote for an Italian-American newspaper in New York. He has been an anti-fascist ever since Mussolini first came to power. In fact, Mussolini was the reason Mike came to America. Mike takes his politics very seriously. Long ago he was beaten up by fascists in Italy and more recently by fascists in New York, and if anybody hates fascists it is Mike, with a sound and seasoned hate. Still, he doesn't want to dump our shipload in the ocean. "We gotta maka da propaganda with the Nazis," he tells me and Jim Youngdale who's in my room shooting the breeze. "We gotta starta da education."

"Mike," I say wearily, "I suppose you want us to put out a newspaper for them and convert them to democracy in two weeks."

"Yes," he says and begins to bounce with eagerness. "Tella dem da trut'."

"One minor point," I say. "The newspaper has got to be in German. Who knows any?" .

Mike's face falls, "You no speaka German?"

"No," I say, *"nicht verstehen."* This isn't strictly true, for I did study German in college and read such things as Goethe's "The Sorrows of Young Werther" and Keller's "Green Heinrich" in the original. Even if I remembered what little German I once knew, it would hardly fill the bill of converting Nazis.

"I know some German," Jim Youngdale says, "I studied it three years in college." So he too read "The Sorrows" and probably "Green Heinrich" also.

Mike is beaming again. "You get out da pape'?" he asks Jim with trust and love.

"We'll try," Jim says.

"Another chore," I say when Mike is gone. "Some of these guys are wonderful at thinking up work for somebody else to do."

"You won't have to bother with it," Jim says. "I'd like to try my hand at it."

"The hell of it is," I say, "it's just what I do want to do and Mike knew it all the time. There isn't much we can accomplish in a couple of weeks but at least we can see whether these Nazis are capable of beginning to think."

"Yeah," Jim says. "We might get something started."

We set to work with the assistance of our bad memories and a War Department pocket manual of German that is full of military terms but strangely omits one we are particularly looking for: "unconditional surrender." A few hours later we have completed the first edition of the *"Amerikanischer Beobachter,"* and posted it in the prisoners' quarters down below. As bad as our German is, it tries to tell them "da trut'" and they crowd to read.

All morning long, every morning, I hold sick

call for the Nazis in the 'tweendecks hospital. The Nazis click their heels at me and refer to me as "Herr Doktor," even after I have the interpreter explain that I am not a doctor but only a make-shift. I have two assistants, Jim Youngdale who volunteers for the experience, and the lanky Nazi boy with the Red Cross bag, who was a first-aid man in the *Arbeitsdienst,* before he became a para-trooper. The interpreter is named Kurt. He is twenty years old and was an officer-candidate in the crack Hermann Goering *Panzerdivision.* Kurt comes from a wealthy Prussian family, with great estates in Estonia and Mecklenburg and a town house in Berlin. Before the war he studied in England. His class-consciousness is acute and he takes a very superior attitude toward the dumb ruck of heel-clicking boys who make up the vast majority of our cargo. He worships the great generals of the *Wehrmacht* and blames Hitler for the military disasters in the East which have made Germany's defeat a certainty. His lip curls at the mention of Goebbels and Himmler. But his German national-ism is firm as a rock, and his family sense. Jim and I half-seriously ask him what he would do if the Americans should fly him back to Germany and parachute him out to organize anti-Nazi resistance.

"I would go home and report to my father for instructions," Kurt says.

Kurt enlarges upon the Bolshevist danger to "civilization" and is mildly amazed when we don't fall in with his views. He is even more surprised when we take issue with his anti-Semitic remarks. He had gathered, he said, that Americans were just as much against the Jews as Germans. Coming across the Mediterranean from Italy, he had got quite intimate with the American Captain of the ship on which he was a prisoner. This Captain had said that most Americans felt Hitler was right about the Jews and only disagreed with some of his methods in handling them.

Seeking some common ground, Kurt opens up confidently on Negroes. In America we have a grave problem, he has heard, with Negroes demanding rights they are incapable of exercising, since as everyone knows they are subhuman and cannot be educated beyond a rudimentary point. His eyes open wide when we tell him that the Captain, Chief Engineer and Chief Mate of this very ship are Negroes, and that his own neck depends on their skill in getting him across the ocean. We tell him who Booker T. Washington was, for whom the ship is named, and Paul Robeson, George Washington Carver, Marion Anderson, Langston Hughes. We ask him if he has heard of the exploits of the 99th Pursuit Squadron in Italy. Kurt falls very silent.

We probe him for his views of the future. He freely admits that Germany has lost the war and that National Socialism will be overthrown. But what next?

"Democracy," he says.

What kind of democracy, we ask him.

"Moderate," Kurt says. "Like in your country."

"Will your father keep his estates?" we ask him.

"Oh yes," he says. "My father is good to his people. And he is good to the twenty-seven American prisoners he has working there. He has nice quarters for them and the British, separate from the Poles and Russians. He lets them go into town on Saturday night."

"What about industry?" we ask him. "Will the same men still own and run it who brought Hitler into power?"

"The good ones will," Kurt says. "Private enterprise is best, don't you think?"

Kurt exclaims with delight over a "Saturday Evening Post" picture of the American armada assembled for the expedition against the Marianas. Hitler made a deplorable error in allying Germany with Japan. "The white race should stick together." Kurt has been hugely impressed with the fighting qualities of American soldiers, the shattering power of our air force and artillery, the inexhaustible quantities of ships, planes, tanks, guns, food—everything—which we have produced and poured overseas.

"It was suicide for us to fight you," Kurt says. "It was all a misunderstanding."

Willi agrees with Kurt on every point. Willi is a Baltic German, from Latvia, who claims to be distantly related to the former Russian Czar. Before the war, he was a professional tennis player and traveled all over Europe. The Jews and the Bolshevists are very bad people, Willi says, as he has seen with his own eyes in Latvia where it was necessary to hang great numbers of them because they persisted in shooting at the German soldiers who came in there to establish order. Even after all the telegraph posts were decorated with hanging bodies of Jews and Bolshevists, the survivors kept on shooting at the German soldiers and sterner measures than hanging had to be adopted. But Willi has a grudge against Germany, too. One night he made a blanc-mange for the officers of his outfit somewhere on the Eastern front. He took it into their headquarters, expecting commendation. Instead, they dashed it to the ground and kicked him in his rear-end, finding the blanc-mange not to their taste. Whereupon, Willi renounced fidelity to Germany in his heart. He intends to settle in America, on Long Island, where he has relatives.

"We don't need you in America," Jim says in halting German. "We've already got too many people with ideas like yours."

Willi just grins, ingratiatingly, and goes on sweeping off the tarpaulin. We can't shake Willi's notion that he will be welcome in America, and that our land will become his future happy home.

For hours on end the sick troop into the little hospital. Each man as his turn comes draws himself up stiff, thrusts out his chin and clicks his heels resoundingly. One kid even gives me the Hitler salute. Kurt grins and taps his head. The kid has peachbloom on his face and looks no more than fifteen. There is something the matter with his ears. They ache all the time. I do the little I know for him and he departs, after heel-clicking and again giving me the Hitler salute. "He doesn't know where he is," Kurt says. "He's been like that ever since he was captured in his first battle. His mind is gone."

Among the boys are a few woebegone men on the edge of middle age. One relic of two years on the Russian front opens a mouth full of pus. Every discernable joint in his body is atrociously swollen— fingers, toes, wrists, ankles, knees, elbows. Somehow he manages to walk. I give him morphine and put him to bed on a heavy course of sulfa. If this man has any desire to go on living, he does not display it. The majority of the patients are covered with horrible boils and carbuncles. The knife and the ethyl chloride "freeze" are in constant use. These men have been trained at least to bear pain, and it is rare for one even to flinch. The bodies of all, spare though they are, are steel-hard.

The middle aged man from near Danzig is utterly dumb the first three or four times he comes to sick call. Then I am sent for to attend him one night when he is having a "sinking spell." Jim comes too. It turns out that all that's wrong with the man is the need to spill his troubles. Talk spouts out of him, bitter and endless. He was a master-miller with a fine mill and three nice houses he owned in the country. Many of the farmers who brought their grain to his mill to be ground were Poles, and he got along with them all right. When the Nazis were out to get the neighborhood Polish priest, he and his father and brothers took him in and sheltered him all one night, sitting up with guns across their knees. The next day the priest got away. Afterwards the Nazis threatened to burn down his houses and his mill unless he lined up with them, so he joined their motor corps. When the war came he kept on running his mill until the attack on Russia. Then the Army removed the mill machinery, saying it was needed at the front. They drafted him into a labor battalion, despite a right arm crippled from boyhood as a result of a mill accident. For two years he worked behind the lines in Russia. Then they transferred him into the infantry, though he couldn't even carry a rifle straight because of his deformity. On his way to Italy, he got a short leave at home. His wife and children were living in one room of one of their three houses. All the rest of the space was occupied by refugees that the Nazis had quartered there from Konigsburg, from Berlin and Essen and Cologne. I ask him if he is worried about what will happen to his family when the Russians, who are poised on the border of East Prussia, get to Danzig.

"Oh, no," he says. "I lived among the Russians for two years. They are just people like us. And what could they take away from me that the Nazis haven't taken already?"

There is the boy whose lip I finally have to cut open to drain out the pus. Like Kurt, he was in the crack Hermann Goering division. He lies in his sick bay bunk reading and rereading a package of letters from home and looking at a sheaf of pictures. These show his village in the Bavarian Alps, his lovely home, his sister and father and mother, the glider club he belonged to, and the prize glider he helped build with a swastika on the tail. Until recently he was a Luftwaffe glider pilot, but since glider pilots are no longer needed, he has been serving as an armored force signalman. He shows me a picture of a hefty young brute in a Luftwaffe uniform. "Who?" I ask him. He points to himself and makes an effort at a smile with his bandaged lip. I have to look and look at the picture and then at his wasted face before I can detect any resemblance. Certainly this buxom mother posed in her garden against the snowy Alps would never know him for her son.

They bring the Austrian to sick call under guard. He is in the brig for the duration of the trip, all by himself behind bars. He was accused by the others of stealing their campaign ribbons at night to trade to the American sailors for cigarettes. He denied it, but requested to be locked up in the brig all the same. He says the others are against him because he's an Austrian. All he wants is to be kept away from them. Before serving on the Italian front as an infantryman, he was a railroad worker on the Russian front, in the Crimea. Did the Germans practice atrocities against the people out there? we ask him. Yes, he says. Did he see them? Yes, he says again. Will he tell us about them? we ask him. No, he says, just put him back in the brig and leave him alone.

The second issue of the *"Amerikanischer Beobachter,"* Jim and I write in English and get Kurt to translate into German. He is quite willing and translates the war news perfectly straight, but when we check back his translation of the editorial on the origins of the war, we find he has distorted it from beginning to end, particularly the part about Hitler and the Jews. Kurt professes to have misunderstood the English, though his English is close to perfect. Again and again we go over the distorted passages and Kurt, with charming apologies for his stupidity, does them over, distorting them still further. We dismiss him and again do our poor best to put down what we mean. To translate the third issue, we call in the SS man.

The first day on deck we picked him out, an aristocratic-looking chap who seemed to have some secret authority over the others and acted as their spokesman. His English is quite adequate. He seems to preside at mess-time, also, and to decide who shall get how much. According to the regulations

of the German Army, the younger soldiers are supposed to get more than the older ones. He spends
a great deal of time around the *"Amerikanischer
Beobachter"* posted on the bulkhead, "interpreting"
our news to the fellows who come up to read. So
when we ask him to translate the third issue, we
are in effect setting a trap for him. We expect him
to distort our meaning even more than Kurt. To
our amazement, he translates it absolutely straight,
even the part about the plan for German war prisoners to work on the reconstruction of the lands
they have destroyed.

The SS man owns a textile mill in Breslau, he
says. Jim and I ask him if he got it from a Jew, and
he begs our pardon, not understanding, so we let
that pass. He seems very nervous and his eyes are
fixed on the shelf over my head, where dangling
down is a piece of rubber hose which I keep there
as an emergency tourniquet. The SS man tells us
about his Russian experience. He went in on June
22, 1941, from Deutsch Eylau in East Prussia, and
fought through the Baltic campaign. In January
he was pushed back by the Russian counterattack
before Moscow. And he claims to have been one of
the handful that escaped from Stalingrad. Despite
these experiences, he has nothing good to say for
the Russian soldier. Americans are far superior,
he maintains, and could easily beat the Russians.
We don't think it will ever come to that, we tell
him. What would we fight them about? He shuts

up. If, we ask him, the Russians are no good as soldiers, what does that make the German soldiers whom they beat before Moscow, at Stalingrad, in the Ukraine and now in Poland?

"You know everything," he says. "How can I tell you anything?"

The SS man starts on a new tack. His fiancée, a good and beautiful girl, is a German WAC in Warsaw. He fears for her safety, now that the Russians are in Praga, just across the river. And he worries over his aged parents in Breslau. "What is going to happen to them? What is going to happen to my home?" He looks at us with real tears in his baby-blue eyes.

"What happened to people's aged parents in Warsaw?" we ask him. "And to their homes? What happened to people and their homes in Russia where you Nazis passed by?"

This is one SS man who's cracking up, we decide. The other Nazi leaders in the group must come to the same conclusion, for our last night out of the United States he is slugged with an iron pipe while asleep in his bunk. They miss his skull, but break his jaw.

The farmer has something wrong with his heart. I try to take his pulse in all the usual places, but can't find it anywhere. Neither can Jim. We can't even get it with the stethoscope. I try his blood-pressure with the sphygmometer. It registers 90/60. I put him to bed in the sick bay while I am wondering what to do with him. Maybe it is battle shock, I think after a while. He is fearfully pale and lifeless with cavernous eyes. Has he ever been wounded? "Yes," he slowly admits. I get him to strip down and itemize the following abnormalities: one crooked elbow, one smashed-up knee, umbilical hernia, eight inch scar on the abdomen with marks of stitches (opposite side from appendix), remainder of abdomen peppered with small scars, mutilated sexual organs. He gives a vague story about it all, accusing a Russian partisan of the sexual mutilation and ascribing the rest to a fall from a hay wagon before the war. But the more I look at the peppering of scars on his abdomen, the more I am reminded of the hobnails on German field boots. We keep pressing and the next day the farmer breaks down and tells the truth.

He has been in the Army since the first of the war. He did well and rose to the rank of mess sergeant. He shows a picture of himself in a mess sergeant's uniform, arm in arm with comrades, under Sicilian palms. He had a soft garrison job there. But he got crossed up with the Nazis in his outfit. They had him busted down to private. He resented it and expressed his hostility even more openly. This landed him in a penal battalion. The small scars on his belly really are the marks of German field boot hobnails, and the umbilical hernia is also a memento of that trampling. The long scar is where they split him open with a gun butt. The crooked elbow and the smashed knee were simply the results of twisting, but the sexual mutilation was done with a red-hot iron. That is what worries him most. Will the American doctors be able to do anything about it so he will be some good again?

While he was in the penal battalion, they worked on his wife at home. They told her he would never get out alive unless she was reasonable and properly entertained the local party members. She came across and when she did, all the details were made fully known to him in the penal battalion, as well as the two pregnancies resulting therefrom.

Kurt, who is translating, is much amused by this part of the story. No woman is any good any more, he says. When he was in Berlin last spring, you could have anybody you wanted.

Having told his story, the farmer feels better, but then he gets terrified all over again. We must promise to keep him in the sick bay all the rest of the trip. And will they take him right to the hospital as soon as the ship docks? He begs us to promise that the Americans will never make propaganda out of his case, never under any circumstances use his name in connection with his story. . . .

The Nazis are putting on an entertainment for us in their prison quarters down below. The hatch boards are taken off and we squat around the open square, looking down. There are boxing matches in which the contestants take roundhouse swings at each other. Kurt, the interpreter, puts on the gloves and shows a little class, but his adversary goes in for him with both arms flailing and punches him groggy. The Nazis roar approval when Kurt is whipped. Songs follow, "Lili Marleen" and others we have never heard. A fellow with a guitar sings a long travelogue about his wanderings to France, Russia, Italy and now at last to "sweet America." The rest take up the last part and chorus their joy at being on their way to sweet America. Cigarettes shower down from the audience and the Nazis scramble for them on the deck below.

Yet there is one quiet, serious guy who never makes advances to the Americans, but sticks to his job of marshaling the prisoners for fire and boat drills, and bossing the work gang which chips the deck. He is the highest-ranking non-com on board. He doesn't have anything to say until nearly the end of the trip. Then he opens up: "Our leaders told us that democracy in America was a fraud. They told us you were hypocritical when you said all men were free and equal. They told us Negroes were no better than slaves in your country. But what we have seen on this ship, the happiness, the comradeship among all of you, your fairness to us when we had been told you would beat and abuse us, all that has made us think. At night, after the lights go out down in the hold, we talk about it, all of us."

CHAPTER TWENTY

Rolling Home

W<small>E</small> <small>ARE ROLLING</small> home light across the great ocean that we have crossed so many times in blue sundrenched calm and gray howl of storm, and in all the nights with the look-outs tense in the blackness, vigilant for the loom of a ship ahead or astern or on our beam, or for the quick white track of a torpedo. The comforting throb of the engines will go on, sixty-eight to the minute, long after I leave the ship for good, and will get her there and back again.

So many men have come, and put what they had into this ship, and have gone as I am going when we arrive in port. But with their leaving, it has not changed, nor will it change with my departure. And those who worked the hardest for our ship, building their memories indissolubly into her, drew far more out of her than they put in. So many good men, so many books they would make if all their stories were told, and how many more good men there will be to come. . . .

That regular throb of the healthy engines brings back to mind the black gang's old chief, Irving Smith, who came out with the ship when she was

first commissioned and stayed with her more than a
year. Whether he was in there swinging a sledge on
engine repairs to show his gang how it should be
done, or whether he was playing host in his quarters
to the AMG officers we were taking overseas, impeccable in his Commander's uniform, nobody did
more to keep us proudly sailing. And many a white
engineer officer will be able to say that he got his
first start up the ladder under this able Negro Engineer whose own climb had been contested at every
rung by prejudice.

Alex Treskin, who came to us as Second Assistant
Engineer, fresh out of upgrading school, for eighteen months poured out all his young energy and
intelligence on his job, and on the bigger job of
making the Booker T. Washington embody the kind
of America he believed in, this son of Russian immigrants who came up from peddling newspapers
on the streets of Frisco, through the brutal blud-
geoning of a seaman's life during the thirties, until
he is now First Assistant Engineer on a crack Victory ship in the Pacific.

The black gang never let us down. Maybe it was
Red Herrick's medallions on the boiler front that
kept them going . . . Larry Burke, the big Boston
Irishman; Fred Deckard, Kentucky white boy and
son of a Chief Engineer, who took orders willingly
and loyally from a Negro superior; George Alafousas, the Greek, whose third war this is; Puerto
Rican Jose Estrella; the big Peruvian, Florentino

Quimper, and that quiet Negro from Brazil who finally broke loose with a big speech at ship's meeting, saying this was the happiest place he had ever been in all the fifty years of his life and all the world should be like our ship some day, and what a big hand he got when Chief Engineer Smith, who understood Portuguese, translated what he had said.

The black gang and the deck were always fighting over which were the most important aboard ship. We had quite a controversy over it in *General Alarm,* our ship's paper, with Alex spokesman for the black gang and Chips the champion of the deck, but it was a draw.

Certainly they don't come any better than Cliff Lastic, who was Second Mate and then Chief Mate with us, coming out with the ship when she was first commissioned. Cliff was a West Indian Negro, like Captain Mulzac, a lad from St. Lucia who followed the example of so many island boys and ran away to sea at thirteen. For many years Cardiff, Wales, was his home port, and he sailed through the First World War on British ships. Afterwards he came to New York and became an American citizen. Nearly every afternoon before he went on watch, Cliff would call me in his room for a spot of tea, which he brewed on his private electric percolator. We talked about politics maybe, or the guys aboard. Like so many essentially serious men, Cliff loved to laugh, and did a lot of it. Often we talked about books for Cliff read constantly and his judgment was good. What he liked most was music, good music. He was always monkeying with the chart-room radio, which is hooked up to loud-speakers over the ship, and trying to get some symphonic or operatic music for a change from jazz. Cliff could identify nearly everything classical he heard. Cliff's bookshelf was lined with navigation books, which he put to such constant use that, when he got his required time in as Chief Mate with us, he tackled the examinations for his master's license. Passing with flying colors, he became skipper of another Liberty, the SS Bert Williams, which is now sailing into the war zones with a mixed crew and applying the same principles which have made the SS Booker T. Washington the kind of ship it is. Cliff is the fourth Negro to command an American ship in this war, the others, besides Captain Mulzac, being Captain Richardson and Captain Godfrey. Only forty-four now, Cliff has many good sea-years ahead of him and it will be a test of America's sincerity to see to it that he continues as a skipper after the war.

Men don't come any better than Cliff Lastic . . . nor any better than Sparks—Chief Radio Operator Cecil Blackman—who could turn your darkest moods inside out with his never-failing merriment. Everything was grist for the mills of his mirth, but his deepest and most gurgling laugh was reserved for the absurd techniques of discrimination practiced against his race.

Sparks was born in British Guiana and brought up as a member of the gentry, being required to wear a stiff collar and a coat in that equatorial clime, to shun public resorts frequented by common persons, and to speak to no one unless properly introduced. Against this early grounding as a member of the master class, he riddled with his laughter the disqualifications to which his black skin later subjected him in the United States. Scrapes with death in the British Navy during the First World War, when his ship sank under him in two minutes flat and he was cast on a mosquito-plagued shore clad only in drawers, made some of his best anecdotage, as well as his years as a henchman of white imperialism in Portuguese East Africa. Here native wives could be purchased for five dollars and returned if the merchandise failed to wear well. Sparks was a supervisor on a sugar plantation there and fanned himself over cool rum drinks in the shade, just like a white man, while the native blacks toiled in the sun. Once on his way across the Zambesi to inspect the merchandise in a native village, his paddlers turned the dugout over and plunged him in the crocodile-infested stream. In painting his own role out there, Sparks drew an exquisite satire on the white lord of the tropics.

Back when Sparks was radio operator on one of Marcus Garvey's Black Star Line ships around 1920, they put into Jacksonville. They had a big dance aboard ship for the local colored population

and it was so successful that they decided to have
another. But they made the mistake of scheduling
it for a Saturday night. The white folks were furi-
ous. It practically killed Saturday night at the club,
for the cooks and maids were all on the ship and
the white folks had to stay home with their own
children for a change. In consequence, the ship's
captain, a Norwegian, was summoned before the
Mayor of Jacksonville. Sparks went with him. In
with the Mayor was a Negro janitor named Morgan.

"You come down here to Jacksonville with this
nigger ship," the Mayor yelled at the Norwegian
captain and Sparks, "trying to stir up all our niggers. Ain't that so, Morgan?"

Morgan straightened up from his sweeping,
"Yassuh, Mr. Mayor," Morgan said, "Thass a
fack."

"Our niggers here in Jacksonville were contented
niggers until you brought that nigger ship in here,"
the Mayor yelled. "Ain't that so, Morgan?"

Morgan stopped wiping off the big brass spitton.
"Yassuh, Mr. Mayor," Morgan said. "Alla us was
contented."

"I'm telling you to get your nigger ship outa here
before sumpn happens to you," the Mayor yelled.

"But we're taking on cargo," the Captain said.

"I don't give a damn," the Mayor yelled. "Get
that nigger ship outa Jacksonville."

"I'll get protection from the federal authorities," the Captain said.

"I'm the federal authorities!" the Mayor yelled, "Ain't that so, Morgan?"

"Yassuh, Mr. Mayor," Morgan said and shuffled his broom a little, "You sho' is all the authorities they is around heah."

The Captain was a hardheaded Norwegian and wouldn't move his ship until the Ku Klux Klan showed up on the pier in their pillow slips and nightshirts. Then he hauled in his gangway and squirted the Klansmen with the ship's firehoses before pulling away from the dock.

Sparks didn't go to sea again from that time until the Booker T. Washington was launched. There just wasn't any ship a Negro operator could get on between 1920 and 1942. In the meantime Sparks had worked up to a good job in the New York Post Office. But when Captain Mulzac asked for him he came back to sea, and he stayed with us nearly two years, dropping off only when the doctor warned him that, with his blood pressure, he might not make it in from another trip. . . .

No, they don't come any better than Sparks Blackman, or old Ben Hammarberg with the gray streaks in his blond Nordic whiskers, so easy-going until somebody in a bar made some crack about his working under a black Bos'n, and it took five guys to drag Ben off the man. Or Herb Kransdorf, the Jewish AB who came back to sea after two years in the Army. Or Nick Arrindell, the slender, intelligent Negro. Or the college boys shipping as ordinaries, Leonard and Skip Schukow and Clark Leavitt and Rosenhouse. They were the boys who wrote pieces for the paper, built up the ship's library until it was the best afloat, served as chairmen and secretaries of ship's meetings, and sat in on all the classes from navigation to engineering and radio.

And all the while the deck and black gang were arguing as to which was the most essential to the ship, the Steward's department kept on feeding us; and never once did they miss serving three hot meals a day, even when we were rolling our rails under, and to fight that galley stove was a peril to life and limb with pots of boiling soup skidding off on the deck and spilled grease flaring up like burning gasoline. On any other ship, you would have got sandwiches on such days, but not on ours. Peter Lee who could cook with the best . . . clumsy Slim who fell over his own feet and yours when he was serving you but came to life on the dance floor and swept through the Lindy hop like some black Ariel . . . Sportin' Life who couldn't write his name but could make cards do things Houdini never dreamed of. When other boys had their noses in books, Sportin' Life was practicing with his cards before the mirror, four and five hours a day. He wouldn't gamble with his shipmates, and when somebody insisted that he get in the game, he would put on a demonstration of how he just couldn't help making those cards perform. After watching it the gamblers were satisfied with his staying out. Sportin' Life specialized in cleaning the wise guys in port, and once he broke the bank in a French joint that had been mopping up on the Americans.

So many more good men there were, and will be, all adding up to the working unity of the SS Booker T. Washington. We are rolling home light now on my last trip, the engines hitting their steady 68-to-the-minute, the look-outs on the bow, the bridge and the stern tense in the blackness, Santiago the Filipino at the wheel, Third Mate Richardson on watch, Captain Mulzac pacing in the darkened wheelhouse, checking on the course. Everybody meshed together, doing the common job.

We were at sea on my first trip when we heard over the radio about the Detroit race riot. It struck us all as something that couldn't possibly have happened, incomprehensible, yet we knew it was true. It didn't make sense for people to be hunting down other people because of the color of their skins, and in America too, as if they didn't have space enough to live together amicably in the ample confines of a big metropolis. Here we were penned up, men of all races and many nationalities, in the narrow quarters of a small ship, under the strain of constant danger, restricted by the blackout to a few crowded fo'c'sles and mess-rooms, yet there was no conflict among us. It ought to be a lot easier even to avoid conflict in all of Detroit, in vast America, in this enormous world. You could never convince anybody who was ever a part of the Booker T. Washington that race conflict is something natural, not engineered by a few to keep the many apart. It is the most natural thing in the world for people to get along, when they are doing a job together.

We hear about the Yalta conference as we are rolling home this time and we aren't surprised that the Big Three reached complete agreement on doing a common job. The spirit of Yalta is just the same as the spirit of our ship and, unlike some people, we have no difficulty understanding it. Another thing we hear about is the successful conclusion of the International Labor Conference in London. The BBC commentator makes a special point about how perfect unanimity was achieved on international labor's objectives for war and peace, in spite of the welter of languages spoken by the delegates and the mixture of races and nationalities represented. The commentator seems to be amazed by this, as if he had for the first time in his life discovered that common men everywhere want the same things. We have known that all along. Language barriers never kept us from getting along with French arsenal workers or Arab stevedores or imprisoned Spanish fighters or starving Italians. These men were our brothers, far easier to understand than the Nazi prisoners who spoke impeccable English, or than the lynchers in our own Detroit.

We don't like to hear people refer to our ship as an "experiment" in race relations. Maybe we are an experiment in staying afloat successfully, in delivering bombs and tanks and soldiers where they are needed, an experiment in the sense that any other wartime ship is one. That is what we have worked at, in the experimental sense, but not at race relations. They took care of themselves, as they would take care of themselves in any other human situation where the same formula was applied, in an armored division, say, or a whole Army, in a big factory, or an entire industry or a city, a state, a nation, a world.

The only proviso is that there must be a common job that everybody is working on. We oughtn't to have to look around to find that. Finishing this war is still such a job. Making a structure of peace that will stay put is still a bigger one, big enough to take our minds off everything else for the next generation. Put it this way to yourself: would you rather have your daughter sitting next to a Negro child in her schoolroom, or would you prefer having her smashed body lugged out of the bombed ruins of the school, as the Negro steward Bradshaw saw in Barcelona, and the terrible vision lingered in his dying eyes? I put it this way to you, because this is the way it is.